AF269438

Seeking Abundance

Design, ecology, and a flourishing planet

Foreword	Lesley Lokko	06

Introduction	Alan Ricks	08

Congo Basin	12

Admiration Across a Distance,
Sarah Mineko Ichioka	54

Harvesting Architecture
from the Site,
Kelly Alvarez Doran	56

Savannah Woodland	58

Beauty for Abundance,
Gaël Ruboneka Vande weghe	64

Metronomic Practice,
Hanif Kara, OBE	154

Strong Women,
Cedric Mizero	158

Afromontane Forest	164

To Present the World Anew,
Anita Berrizbeitia	232

Learn, Create, and Inspire,
Dieuveil Malonga	234

Afterword	Sierra Bainbridge	236

Acknowledgments	238

Seeking Abundance: Design, Ecology, and a Flourishing Planet

Every so often—and less frequently than one might imagine—a practice comes along, introduces itself to a wider audience through publications and award-schemes, and hunkers down to the serious business of delivering projects. And the dial suddenly shifts. Terms that were familiar or taken for granted, change. Over the past decade on the African continent, several practices have emerged that redefine what we mean by the term "architect" and what we might reasonably expect from a group of professionals who join forces in order to build. Chief among those is MASS, a group of built environment professionals working in over twenty countries around the world, primarily and notably in Africa. Their impact has been felt in too many places to count, but from where I'm sitting in Accra, Ghana, it's their African work—driven primarily by their Rwandan office—that stands out in relation to the theme of this book, *Seeking Abundance*.

Africa is typically framed through the lens of lack—of resources, capacity, skills, opportunity. We speak of abundance mostly in relation to minerals and raw materials, invisible seams of raw profit that lie mostly beneath the surface of our land or in our lakes and seas. Many of the minerals on which the modern world depends have no name in any African language. What was silicon before Berzelius?

The term "seeking" implies a desire to go beyond façade and lazy cliché, to examine conditions, contexts, cultures, and collaborations that might foster new ways of seeing and building that are specific to here but replicable and relevant all over the world. An invitation (and opportunity) to write the foreword for a book about abundance in the African context seldom comes around. It's a rare opportunity to think more deeply about how we frame the word "abundance," how we celebrate it, and, crucially, what steps are needed to ensure it is not only understood in terms of profit or material accumulation, but equally in terms of justice, equity, and generosity. This book is therefore about abundance of a different sort: ambition, hope, energy, empathy. Its origins lie far beneath the surface of the individual projects on display. They lie in the firm's name (Model of Architecture Serving Society), its organizational structure, its locations and its leadership team, its commitment to research, practice, and teaching—an abundance of ideas about how a global office can work both locally and intimately without losing global reach and relevance. Lessons learned in one context can be applied and adapted elsewhere. The dynamics between Africa and the Global North are always complex and often fragile. MASS's emphasis on lessons, on learning and listening is important: Rather than a solutions-driven approach that favors transplanting models from elsewhere onto Africa, the decision to invest in Rwanda not just as a source of projects and problems-to-be-solved but as a center of innovation and ideas is both unusual and underplayed. Architectural education and architectural projects have different (though usually complementary) timescales. Education is invariably a one-generation undertaking, with results only emerging or evident a decade or so down the line—at best. Projects can have anything from a 12-to-36-month timescale; shorter and more immediate, in other words. It is a rare practice that will commit to a long-term educational enterprise, particularly in the first couple of decades of its founding. Under the umbrella of "research," MASS's list of initiatives is impressive, from books to "labs" to tools. Tellingly—and this is perhaps symptomatic of the larger questions around education's relationship to practice—educational initiatives are described as training, one area that deserves reframing.

Foreword

**by
Lesley Lokko**

Whilst architects do undoubtedly train to qualify as professionals, the term doesn't do justice to the abundance of ambition and vision of the company's set-up that anticipates not only their own needs but, importantly, those of the wider society. In a country of fourteen million people, Rwanda has only one school of architecture. In the world's fastest-urbanizing continent, however, the need for more built environment professionals is exponentially greater, graver, and more urgent.

Visit any African capital city and you are likely to find a thriving transport network owned and operated not by the state or the municipality, but by private (and often multiple) owners. In the absence of large public transportation schemes—buses, underground/overground trains, trams, and so on—private taxis, minivans, small buses, and motorcycles transport hundreds of thousands of workers daily. Unlike latecomers Uber and Bolt, the slogans stencilled on windows and occasionally side panels are more often deeply philosophical rather than corporate. "Save money: better girls are coming." "Don't talk, just act." "Good name is better than money." One that stands out from my own childhood, less seen nowadays is, "Paddle your own canoe." As a phrase, its first known usage in the English language dates from the 1844 children's novel *The Settlers in Canada* by Frederick Marryat. However, as is often the case, the proverb has existed in many African languages for centuries. It's an apt metaphor for contemporary African urbanity: The building of a canoe is always a team effort, involving many artisans, but you will undertake the journey alone. Into this precarious context MASS has inserted another, different paradigm: Both the making of the vehicle (practice) and the making of the methodologies (projects, teaching, research, training) are team efforts, conceived, practiced, and executed in different locations but using the base leadership and organizational structure as the support. In contexts like ours, where the infrastructure on which successful initiatives rely is lacking, this is almost revolutionary in its approach—an abundance of support and enabling practices that allow ambition to flourish and ideas to take hold.

The book covers three projects, all located in Africa, and prioritizes four principles by which to live and design: ecology, engineering, regeneration, and respect. The case studies are rural or landscape-based but the principles extend far beyond the forests and wetlands. To fulfil the mandate established in the first instance by the architects, the practice has grown to incorporate contractors, tradespeople, artisans, and artists. The supply chain of ephemeral labor (ideas, concepts, dreams) and material labor (resources, capital, infrastructure) involved in bringing a project to life is long and circuitous. MASS's investment in understanding the full scope of the supply chain in its full complexity and full life cycle has given it unusual agency over the process and outcome. In the introduction to the book, the authors speak of a future where "abundance is possible," but I would argue that it is already here.

Lesley Lokko is a distinguished Ghanian-Scottish architect, educator, and best-selling novelist. She is the founder and director of the African Futures Institute, established in Accra, Ghana, in 2020, as a postgraduate school of architecture, research center, and public events platform. In 2015, she founded the Graduate School of Architecture at the University of Johannesburg.

Abundance is not measured by accumulation, but by equilibrium—when all species, including our own, thrive in relation to one another.

Defining Abundance to Meet this Global Moment

It has never been clearer that people's and the planet's prosperity are inseparable. When biodiversity is threatened and eradicated, we face catastrophic outcomes, including plague, famine, and fire, testing our resilience. But, when biodiversity is nurtured and balanced, people and the planet may heal and, indeed, prosper. As designers, we must confront the urgent need to prevent the former and nurture the latter.

Abundance has been a guiding philosophy for MASS for many years now, and, as a word, it has been enjoying a significant amount of media attention lately, proffering different definitions. One thing is certain: Abundance does not mean limitless. It does not mean a surfeit, and it does not mean bountiful. Abundance is balance. In ecological terms, a species becomes abundant when it maintains a stable population that coexists in harmony with its surroundings. Achieving this balance means operating within limits, neither overexploiting resources nor becoming overly scarce. An abundant ecology fosters biodiversity and resilience.

In *Seeking Abundance*, we explore how design can embrace these ecological principles to create a future where both people and the planet can flourish. As communities worldwide face mounting challenges—climate threats, social inequities, and resource scarcity—the role of design has never been more critical. We must move beyond the goal of doing less harm and instead pursue a future where all people and ecosystems thrive in balance. This belief forms the foundation of our thesis: Abundance is possible when design aligns with the needs of both people and the planet.

At MASS (Model of Architecture Serving Society), we take on projects challenging the status quo. As a global, multidisciplinary collective, we leverage the intersectionality of our team and work to maximize every project's potential. We lift narratives of culture, craft, and beauty to remind us of the links that bind us to one another. This book reflects that ambition.

Communities worldwide are grappling with immense challenges, from pandemics and colonization's legacies to housing shortages and climate change threats. Too often, the role of the built environment is overlooked when seeking to understand and address these intersecting and entangled inequities.

The path forward lies between two critical boundaries, as described by economist Kate Raworth in her concept of Doughnut Economics: a social foundation and a planetary ceiling. Within these boundaries exists a just and sustainable space where humanity—and the planet—can thrive. Establishing a social foundation means we ensure that every person has access to basic conditions for dignity and opportunity. The planetary limits refer to the nine boundaries safeguarding Earth's ecological systems, which Johan Rockström and other leading scientists established. These ideas are gaining traction in the design discourse and have resulted in the development of guides and tool kits like the open-source guide and tool kit *Doughnut for Urban Development*.

Introduction by Alan Ricks

Over the past few decades, the design and construction industries have primarily focused on reducing operational energy use in buildings—an essential step yet insufficient to address the broader and more holistic impacts of our decisions. To go further, we must imagine what it means to achieve net-zero impact and regenerate the planetary systems we depend on.

Regeneration applies to the landscapes we build upon and inhabit and to the broader landscapes touched by design and construction processes. A holistic understanding includes the origins of raw materials, their methods of extraction, transportation, and assembly, and the entire life cycle impact of the buildings themselves. However, the lack of transparency within supply chains makes this incredibly challenging to account for.

And even if we succeed in significant reductions in embodied carbon, the reality remains that construction, by its very nature, will still leave an environmental footprint. Mitigation will always be insufficient and require complementary conservation and ecological regeneration efforts to balance the negative impacts of construction. The active stewardship of forests, waterways, soils, and other natural systems is foundational to sustainable development in the face of escalating climate crises.

The Anthropocene is a Turning Point

We live in the Anthropocene—a geologic epoch that represents a profound change stemming from the direct result of human impact. Climate change, acidifying oceans, and habitat destruction are but a few of the unintended consequences of decades of exploitation of Earth's resources. The Holocene, the epoch that preceded it, spanned over eleven thousand years and was marked by relative climatic stability. However, the mid-twentieth century ushered in what scientists call the "Great Acceleration," a period of unprecedented growth in population and resource extraction that yielded soaring levels of atmospheric carbon, methane, and nitrogen, as well as widespread biodiversity loss.

For decades, scientists such as Donella Meadows have forewarned of these challenges, notably in the 1972 publication *Limits to Growth*. Rockström's latest findings reveal that humanity has transgressed six of the nine planetary boundaries, pushing critical Earth systems toward potential collapse. We are now approaching, and in some cases have already crossed, tipping points, thresholds beyond which environmental damage may become irreversible.

Agriculture has arguably led to the most significant human-driven transformation of the planet. While it has supported growing populations, it has also introduced destructive processes such as deforestation and soil erosion. These impacts extend beyond food security, contributing to the rise of pandemics, among other things. Recognizing these interconnections is crucial to designing solutions supporting human well-being and environmental health.

A New Paradigm for Design

Our work over the past decade, primarily in East Africa, has demonstrated that a new paradigm for design is not only possible but essential. This view begins with the principle of One Health, which was first developed in the field of public health and acknowledges that human, animal, and ecosystem health are inextricably linked. This holistic view demands that we think critically about the provenance of the materials we use, the systems we design, and the broader ecological impacts of our work.

This book is structured around three chapters, each centered on a distinct ecology and case study project: the Ilima Primary School in the Congo Basin, the Rwanda Institute for Conservation Agriculture (RICA) in the savannah woodland, and the Ellen DeGeneres Campus of the Dian Fossey Gorilla Fund in the Afromontane Forest. Each chapter explores the challenges and opportunities unique to these ecologies and presents transformative projects that embody the principles of regenerative design.

The Ilima Primary School is an extraordinarily unique project. Located deep in the jungle of the Democratic Republic of the Congo, the Ilima community is one of the most isolated in the world. For generations, the people of Ilima have coexisted with now-endangered wildlife in the surrounding forest. Still, this fragile ecosystem has suffered due to population growth, migration, mining, and resource extraction. Many of the principles we learned from this project stemmed from the constraint of only being able to work with immediately available resources and have influenced the way we think about material selection and construction methods that celebrate craft and culture. Andrew Brose, the architect who led the project, moved there with his wife, Rachel. He oversaw the design and construction and demonstrated an extraordinary commitment to advancing these ambitions.

In addition to these case studies, each chapter features a photo-essay capturing the essence of ecology, along with data visualization and writing by Gaël Ruboneka Vande weghe. Gaël, a scientist, entrepreneur, and artist who grew up in Rwanda, brings a personal perspective through his photography and writing shaped by his experiences in some of Central Africa's most pristine yet fragile natural environments.

Reflecting our multidisciplinary approach at MASS, this book also illustrates the broad scope of our work, from the scale of furniture to the scale of ecosystems. To effect change at this level, we have taken on unprecedented scope and risk. We established our own construction company, employing over 2,500 people to ensure ethical, safe practices and to maintain agency over the supply chain. We built all three of the projects featured in this book. Our team includes scientists, architects, industrial designers, engineers, researchers, filmmakers, and graphic designers, all working together to realize these projects. While there are far too many to name individually here, we've endeavored to expansively include these perspectives and the diversity and depth of their work through the case studies and chapters of the book.

To address the planetary crisis, we must advance regenerative practices throughout the design and construction process. This means adopting practices that prioritize biodiversity, carbon sequestration, and ecological resilience.

As designers, we have a unique ability to shape the future and shape it into a just and regenerative one. Through the lens of rewilding, conservation, and innovation, we invite you to imagine a future where the places we design are sustainable and profoundly regenerative, a future where the balance that abundance signifies is possible.

**Congo
Basin** Ilima

The village of Ilima in the Democratic Republic of the Congo is home to a groundbreaking educational initiative, an ecologically conscious school that addresses the twin challenges of improving rural childhood education and conserving threatened biodiverse ecosystems. The Ilima Primary School is a key part of the African Wildlife Foundation's "Classroom Africa" program to encourage the next generation of conservationists of both human and natural resources. MASS designed a living platform for education, conservation, and community resilience, drawing most of its materials from a ten-kilometer radius and creating jobs in this part of eastern Befale Territory.

The Ilima Primary School, situated six hours by motorcycle from the closest airstrip, is within the world's most ecologically rich yet vulnerable regions: the Équateur Province of the Democratic Republic of the Congo (DRC). Once part of the Congo Free State, King Leopold II's personal colony, the region bears the legacy of colonial exploitation of people and natural resources, particularly through rubber and timber extraction. In 1908, the Congo Free State became a colony of Belgium, which continued these exploitative practices and failed to develop strong educational or governance systems for Congolese citizens. There were fewer than twenty Congolese university graduates in the entire country in 1960, the year the Democratic Republic of the Congo secured its independence. Today, expanding palm oil plantations, mining, agriculture, and rapid population growth threaten the Congo Basin, the second-largest rainforest in the world, which is losing nearly five hundred thousand hectares per year.

This forest is also home to the bonobo, a deeply social, peaceful, and matriarchal great ape species found nowhere else on Earth. Bonobos face increasing threats from habitat fragmentation, bushmeat hunting, and weak legal enforcement, pressures compounded by regional instability and climate change. The continuous forest canopy critical to bonobo survival continues to disappear as agricultural fields, roads, and settlements expand their reach.

Economic and food security remains elusive for many people in the DRC despite the region's immense biodiversity. Many communities rely on agricultural and sustenance practices that, when compounded, can undermine long-term human sustainability. In remote villages like Ilima, where average incomes often fall below $1 per day, the opportunity to pursue education is limited. According to the World Bank in 2015, only 67.5 percent of the population had completed primary school. Those that do attend are often in dark, poorly ventilated classroom shelters or under trees with few desks or chalkboards, and teacher retention is a persistent challenge.

In 2012, the African Wildlife Foundation (AWF) partnered with MASS to address this complex intersection of conservation and community development. Through its African Conservation Schools program, AWF sought to empower local communities living at the edge of endangered ecosystems by investing in conservation education. In exchange for a commitment to protect intact habitat rainforest from hunting and agricultural expansion, AWF proposed building a durable, well-lit, and ventilated school that would anchor a broader environmental curriculum. Completed in 2015, Ilima reflects MASS's commitment to human-centered, contextually responsive, and environmentally conscious design, galvanizing principles it had been cultivating for years, and laying the groundwork for future projects like the Rwanda Institute for Conservation Agriculture and the Dian Fossey Gorilla Fund's campus.

MASS conducted an in-depth pre-design immersion to understand Ilima's specific needs—interviewing residents, observing daily life, and leading focus groups with local youth. The resulting design for Ilima Primary School responded directly to this research by providing not just a physical building but also a living platform for education, conservation, and community resilience. By targeting primary education, especially important in a country with one of the world's youngest populations, the school offers children a viable alternative to slash-and-burn farming or bushmeat hunting. It equips them with knowledge of ecology, sustainable agriculture, and conservation, and helps unlock future opportunities as forest rangers, wildlife guides, or stewards of ecotourism.

The Ilima School alone cannot solve the systemic challenges facing the Congo Basin, but as a replicable model at the intersection of human, wildlife, and landscape ecologies, it demonstrates how conservation and education can reinforce each other. By integrating habitat protection with educational investment, the project offers a hopeful path forward, one rooted in place, shaped by community, and oriented toward long-term ecological balance.

Impact Beyond Education: Cultivating Human and Natural Resources

A conversation about striking new balances at Ilima, a school whose remote location challenged MASS to harvest most of the building from the site, the basis of both curricular and community impact.

PG   The Ilima Primary School was part of a larger initiative by the African Wildlife Foundation to develop a series of conservation schools across the continent in key environmentally vulnerable areas where they were working to protect wildlife. Ilima sits in the middle of the Congolese jungle and is home to the endangered bonobo apes and their habitat. AWF saw that protecting this species and ecosystem would depend on the support and stewardship of the local community. The community valued education and the opportunity it would provide their children. Their existing classroom space was informal, a lean-to-type roof structure with no protection from the elements. In this condition, there was an opportunity for mutual benefit and shared goals between AWF and the community—AWF would provide a school building and conservation education, and the community would protect the thousands of acres of rainforest from hunting, logging, and extractive agriculture. My role at MASS at the time was as a designer, working across our projects with AWF conservation schools on the continent. There was one in Ethiopia and another one in Tanzania. And so, in each context, we had to understand the unique qualities and tensions between human development and wildlife conservation and how design and the school construction needed to uniquely respond.

AB   I'd been part of that broader community, living in the Democratic Republic of the Congo's region for a long time, and the country has been largely left to its own devices, also for a long time. It's been really struggling since independence in the 1960s. I've always wanted to figure out a way to bring some of my skills to work there with an agency that had the right intentions from the outset in terms of engaging with the community to understand how building infrastructure, specifically education, could have a long-lasting impact. I like working with my hands and most architects don't get to build things with their hands, and so this was a good opportunity to go try to put clay and wood together.

Shifting Design's Lexicon Toward Society's Needs

PG   Before we even put pencil to paper, the project started with deep engagement. Sierra and Andrew traveled to Ilima and immersed themselves in the community, working with AWF, the community, parents, and the current teachers and students, to really fully understand their ambitions, desires, and hopes for the school. They also dedicated time to understanding the opportunities for construction—the skills, talents, and resources available locally, but also the very real constraints.

AB   The two main structures of Ilima are designed as two arcs, which symbolize the twin missions of the school, conservation and agriculture. From a practical standpoint, we had to figure out how we were going to put these arcs on the ground, how we'd measure them, and where the arcs would extend into space, and you're not dealing with typical surveying equipment. We had to figure out how to build it, and the most straightforward way was to draw arcs against two points that you just pull a radius from, and that's kind of the story of the project, an idea for this balance between the natural or wild, and the curated or the crafted.

PG   The location of Ilima being so remote, taking two flights over two days and six hours by motorcycle from the closest airstrip for the team to visit, we had to think about how people, materials, and tools were going to get there, things that were going to have to be shipped months in advance, then floated up the river, and then taken on a six-hour motorbike ride to the site. We made an intentional decision early on in the design that building materials would need to come from within walking distance of the site. We worked with conservation experts to identify trees that could be sustainably harvested and transformed into boards, and leveraged local ingenuity to use traditional practices like using soil from termite mounds as the material for earth blocks. Everything that we couldn't find locally had to be measured precisely, and the logistics of its transport to the site were mapped very thoughtfully. There was so much planning that went into the design; we not only drew a detail on paper but then had to translate it into creating the entire bill of quantities, deciding months before construction began how many bolts we were going to need and how many meters of metal wire would be required to attach the shingles. Minimizing the amount of imported materials was not only a practical one but created additional micro-economies in the community, and repairs, replacements, or additions could be managed locally as well. In this way, the craft of building a school like Ilima is not just a design experiment or short-term investment but a part of the community in perpetuity. Working within ecological limits didn't mean reducing ambition, it meant redefining it. Abundance, here, came not from excess but from interconnection with place.

AB   I'll make two points about this term "craft." First, the handprint of the builder is really evident here. I think that one reason the project has gained so much attention is because the craft is noticed. The second point is really about the tools and the skills that existed here. We understood what they were, and there were limitations to the tools we had available and to the skill sets that were available. We had to bring in some additional tools. We had to make some of our own tools. And those two things, the skill and the tool, again, influenced how this building went up because that's what we had. We talk about craft as if it was intentional, and in some ways, it was, but for the most part, it had to do with what we had available to us.

PG   Despite Ilima's constraints, we were resolved to create a building for this community that went beyond what was the most convenient or straightforward solution. The building design, as Andrew mentioned, was generated from two arcs that symbolize the intersection between conservation and agriculture, but then, sitting on top of the arc walls are these ambitiously scaled handmade trusses installed radially, and they resolve into this dynamic and almost parabolic roof that connects the two sides together. I reflect sometimes on the audacity of the design—and how important it was for this building to communicate something more than the bare minimum and to be more than a structure.

AB   Ilima doesn't look like the standard, prototypical school design for this region, and it became a point of pride, something that was recognized by the Ministry of Education, which allocated additional resources to it. People recognized this extra meaning behind the design, and they started asking questions, demanding their kids go to this school, demanding there are proper resources and funding from the ministry, that teachers were compensated, and that their qualified teachers come to the school. And that kind of process of working with the community to develop a design, which is representative of a place, is ultimately, I think, what we've tried to do through all of our work.

PG   That's part of the evolution of MASS, too. I mean, I would say Ilima is where I learned a lot that benefitted projects like Fossey, which sits on the edge of the national park and sought to restore agricultural land for the protection of gorillas. It's interesting to think about these two projects, both with partners who were established in the 1960s specifically to protect wildlife, and how architecture and design have been used to help them communicate their investment not only in conservation but in the communities that surround them.

AB   Initially, we had set out with this idea that there's wildlife and ecology, both of which need to be preserved and cared for, but sustainable development also means dedicated farmland and agricultural practices, and that kind of balance is actually really healthy from a land preservation standpoint. And it's also really good for you not to just be eating cassava or maize, but also to be finding things that are grown naturally in the environment. But that requires balance and understanding. That mindset is something that attaches to Ilima and has also attached to other MASS projects, and it's a mindset that is uncommon in lots of other parts of the developing world.

PG   This project also challenges our understanding of and reverence toward materials, toward labor, and of only taking from the earth what we need. As a society, we have lost perspective on how materials are made and, for example, what it actually takes to make a piece of lumber. In the films and photos we have from Ilima, anyone can see the scale of the tree that was cut down, how many people it took to move it, how intensive it was to see those boards, plane them, and exactly how many boards or shingles each produced. While Andrew was on-site for construction, we would talk weekly to give updates on the construction project, but for months often our only update was the tracking of materials; the number of boards, bricks, and shingles that had been made. It made the labor, which is often invisible or opaque in our typical supply chains, visible. It made it so clear to me how much of architecture and construction relies on the availability of materials, yet in North America and other parts of the world architecture practice is limited to selecting materials from a catalog. Ilima shows us an alternative and a means to find balance in our profession as well.

AB   I think we are constantly inspired by the story within the architecture community of Ilima because it distills a lot of these ideals that we have as a practice and as a profession for what it means to do architecture and for what it means to do it in a way that is purpose-built. Most of the people who were working on this project were not thinking about the architecture. They were thinking about the economic opportunity. Ilima has influenced our own trajectory as a practice and how we've moved forward with projects like RICA.

Patricia Gruits
Co-Executive Director, MASS

Andrew Brose
Director, MASS

The Ilima Primary School campus fosters mutually beneficial habitats for its students, instructors, and the local ecology. In 2012, MASS began work with the AWF in the Equator Province of the Democratic Republic of the Congo, where the organization was focused on preserving biodiversity, specifically the endangered bonobo species. The region presented clear tensions between population growth, agriculture, and conservation. Although the program was for a school, the broader brief was for a community asset that could achieve the balance rooted in abundance with a minimal impact on the local ecology. MASS sourced nearly all its materials from the surrounding landscape; 94 percent from within a ten-kilometer radius. Builders worked alongside conservationists to harvest local trees for structural members, collect termite mound soil for adobe bricks, and gather reeds for doors and screens. MASS designed Ilima to integrate seamlessly with its environment, bridging agricultural land and dense forest, and offering children spaces that inspire exploration, imagination, and ecological awareness.

AWF sought to reduce habitat encroachment by supporting communities living on the margins of bonobo territory through investments in conservation education. MASS envisioned the school itself as a threshold between forest and farmland—a living laboratory where students could study forest ecology and explore improved agricultural techniques. The steep roof and gutter system drew from local, climate responsive design traditions, designed to manage heavy rainfall while providing shelter from both sun and rain in communal areas. Paired with an open clerestory, the design maximizes natural ventilation and daylight, ensuring comfortable classroom environments. The surrounding landscape features play equipment made with local materials and methods, as well as integrated habitat zones and on-site community agricultural testing and research. MASS placed educational signage throughout Ilima's grounds, turning the campus into an immersive learning environment that utilizes AWF's wildlife conservation curricula.

The campus design emphasizes flexibility and adaptability through open learning spaces. MASS arranged classrooms around a central courtyard, fostering connections across age groups and subjects. Ilima was designed as a hub of activity, serving vital community functions beyond the curriculum, while remaining ready to meet its core educational mission across any subject. The school became not just a center of learning, but one of ecological equilibrium; its open plan, adaptive systems, and rootedness in the landscape formed an architecture of balance.

The project's impact extended to the local labor force, as well. MASS employed 120 workers from Ilima's eastern Befale Territory, 20 percent of them women, and injected significant financial resources into the region. Its environmentally conscious construction produced 307,000 kilograms fewer carbon emissions than the global average for a school of similar size. Since opening, Ilima has drawn students from five villages within a 23-kilometer radius, contributing to increased enrollment and a remarkable 95 percent pass rate on primary school exit exams. Each year, the school welcomes over 1,200 users, including students, teachers, and visitors.

By intertwining education and conservation, Ilima serves as both a beacon of learning and a model for sustainable development in rural Africa. It offers a radical proposition: that abundance can be hand-built, hyperlocal, and deeply reciprocal. This is not abundance defined by scale or finish but by interdependence, balancing local materials with cultural continuity, and community aspiration with ecological stewardship. Ilima redefines what it means to build with ecological and social balance. Its value lies not only in how little was taken, but in how much was returned, to students, to craftspeople, and to the surrounding rainforest. It demonstrates how education, labor, and biodiversity can thrive together, not in opposition but in harmony, and reminds us that education, when rooted in place, can be a strategy for planetary healing.

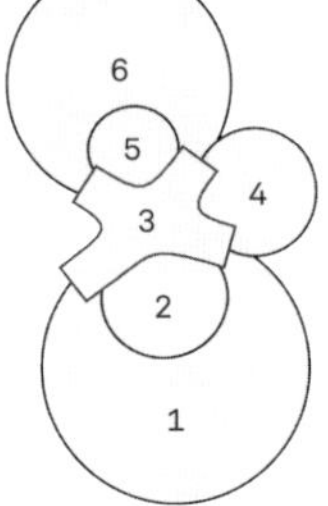

1.   Agriculture
2.   Community
3.   School
4.   Entry
5.   Play
6.   Habitat

Regenerative Design for a Remote Community

Ilima's six
instructional spaces,
administrative
office, and library
are oriented and
optimized for natural
ventilation and
circulation.

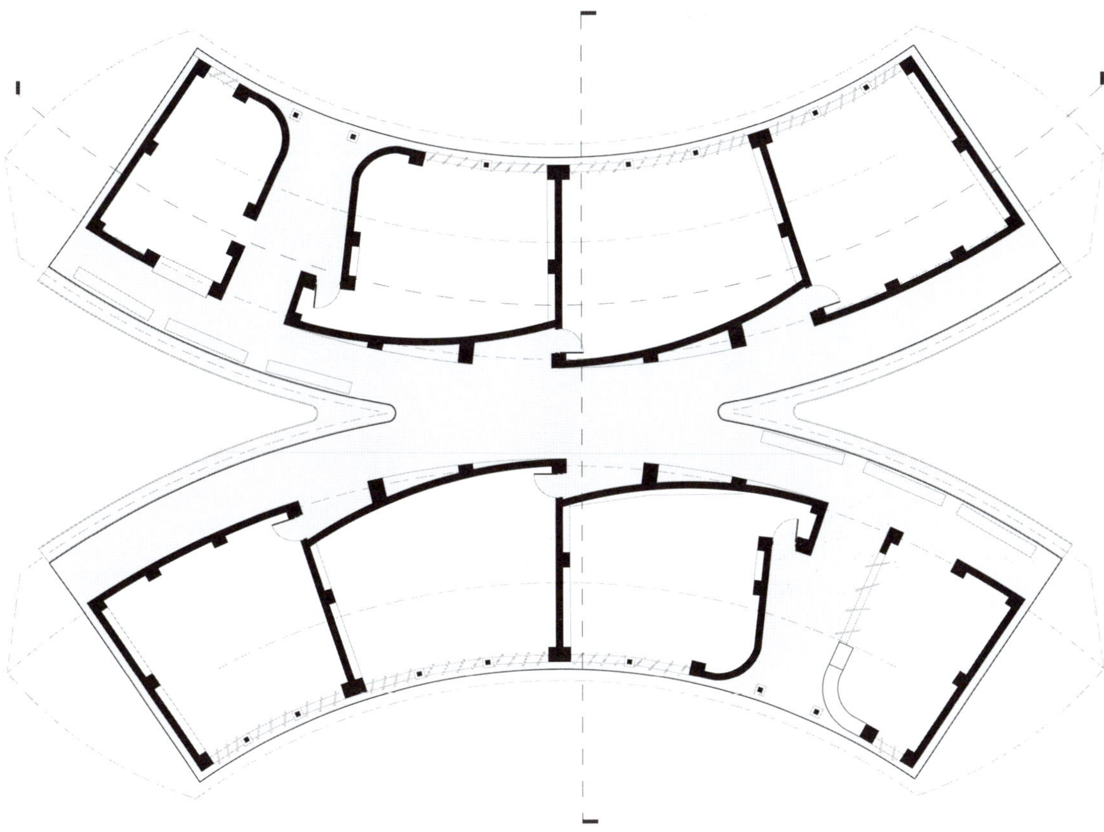

Each of the trusses
were constructed on-
site by newly trained
carpenters from the
nearby towns of Djolu,
Mopono, and Boende.

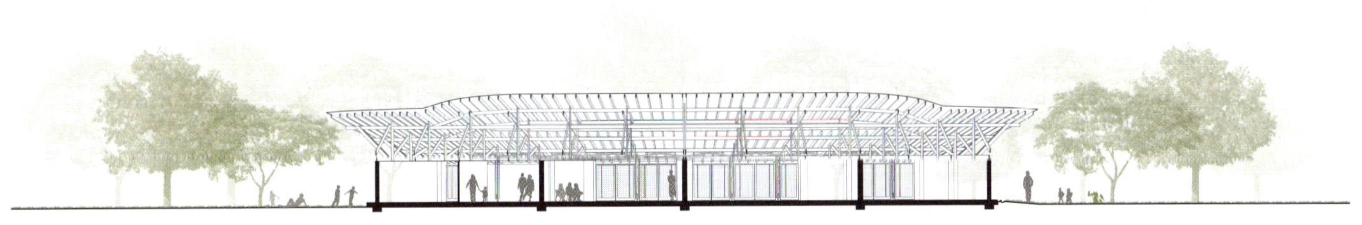

Although remote, the village of Ilima is rich in natural resources, skilled craftspeople, and a deep tradition of building. These advantages became central to the vision for a new school—one rooted in place and created by the community.

To understand both what the community needed and desired, as well as how to build in this remote place, the pre-design process included immersive fieldwork in Ilima, alongside visits to Kinshasa, the capital, and Djolu, a town six hours away by motorbike and home to the nearest office of the AWF, the project's lead partner. This fieldwork was critical to shaping Ilima's physical form, as well as its potential as a symbol of regenerative landscape on the continent. MASS observed the community's relationship with the existing school, learned about its aspirations for the new campus, and identified opportunities for the construction process to generate lasting local benefit beyond the final building. Conversations and community meetings with teachers, students, and parents revealed the community's desire for a "campus" that could educate students and provide sorely needed meeting spaces for other groups in the community. Conversations with the village's masons, brickmakers, and transporters revealed the skill sets and talents within the community that MASS could call upon to create a workforce, and use to identify solutions for greater material durability.

Conversations about timber framing and furniture fabrication led us to two master carpenters in Djolu, Camile Abiyo and Papa Daniel Isekiyoko, experts not only in felling, sawing, and planing timber but also in vannerie, a local weaving technique.

Ilima residents guided the team to nearby forests to examine deposits of clay, sand, and stone, and shared traditional methods for enhancing earthen construction. One technique used termite-processed soil to increase the strength of sunbaked bricks. We documented these fabrication methods and collected material samples for further analysis. On another forest walk with the village's mothers, we learned about the trees and plants that were often utilized for food or for their ethnobotanical value. For instance, the sapelli and tali trees host a highly sought-after edible caterpillar that is

Conducting Fieldwork to Lay the Groundwork

by Andrew Brose & Sierra Bainbridge

both nutritious and tasty and serves as a staple food as well as a source of income, but often the trees are cut down to harvest the crop, over time endangering this protein source that most families rely on. Incorporating such local knowledge, tree and plant lists were created, which tracked their material, food, and medicinal uses.

Given the challenges of transportation and the prolific possibilities shared by the community, we suddenly realized that the entire school building could, and should, be sourced directly from this place, much like the vernacular homes, but with improved durability and the reduced burden of seasonal maintenance. These early visits, guided walks, and curious conversations revealed the richness of both material culture and resources that could be carried into this new educational infrastructure. This informed a design that culminated in eighteen months of collaborative construction, with carpenters, weavers, masons, and laborers. The result was more than just a building, it was a living testament to the value of local knowledge, ecological stewardship, and shared purpose in creating lasting infrastructure.

Congo
Basin
Ilima

**Stepping Gently into
a Micro-Economy**

Relearning How to Build

Collaborating with Termites

Weaving a New Future

Every Cut Considered

Craft as a Living Legacy

Framing the Story

Building locally means not only maximizing long-term benefits for a community, but also carefully considering how a project can support the local economy without destabilizing it.

Once MASS understood that the long-term viability of a building depended on its ability to be maintained through a local market, which would need to be established for construction, it became clear that the design would need to align with a supply chain rooted in proximate, familial, and communal material sourcing. We were tapping into the richness of Ilima's commons to create a generational community asset. By linking the design intimately to the landscape of available materials, a micro-economy emerged specifically around the procurement of building resources.

Despite the vastness of the forest, land and trees in Ilima were well accounted for, each parcel and tree associated with specific families. Rights to individual trees were typically exchanged for labor. In return for felling and milling a tree, builders would keep offcuts or sapwood boards. A similar system governed other materials, with transportation priced by volume and distance, creating a dynamic market for delivery and logistics. The majority of materials reached the site by foot, having been cut, dug, woven, or produced on or near Ilima. Some were carried by bicycle, including the palm oil used to seal bricks and wall plaster, which traveled two hundred kilometers from a factory in Boende.

To manage the flow of goods, daily prices were posted on a chalkboard outside the site. A market of harvesting, production, and transportation blossomed just beyond the gates. Materials were delivered and deposited in "cabbage," or cubic volumes tallied and tracked as a kind of physical banking system. This allowed us to trace every component of the building by source, time, and cost, making it possible to quantify the embodied energy required for production, and to understand the direct economic investment the project made in the community.

The ratio between material and labor costs varies globally. In developed economies, labor is often the largest expense, while in developing contexts like Ilima, materials and energy typically dominate budgets. Living alongside the procurement and construction of this building yielded tremendous insight into how to minimize destructive aspects of the building process, while maximizing potential for abundance and agency for the communities involved. Ilima has influenced the trajectory of MASS's practice, becoming the stepping-off point for scaling and elaborating on this way of working through later projects like RICA and Fossey.

Stepping Gently into a Micro-Economy

by Sierra Bainbridge

IMPLICATIONS OF SPECIFYING MATERIALS FOR ILIMA	THATCH	HARDWOOD	METAL	TILE-FIRED	BAMBOO
Lifespan without maintenance, years	0.5	3–5	8–10	10	0.5
Lifespan with maintenance, years	1–2	20–100	8–10	20–30	1–2
Maintenance, relative effort	3 figures	3 figures	1 figure	2 figures	3 figures
Structural complexity	Easy	Medium	Easy	Hard	Medium
Labor, relative effort	2 figures	4 figures	1 figure	3 figures	2 figures
Replicability for the region	High	High	Low	Medium	Medium
Dependency on AWF	1 elephant	2 elephants	4 elephants	3 elephants	1 elephant
Cost	▪	▫▪	▫▪█	▫▪▪	▪
Local availability	helicopter	1 plane	2 planes	1 plane	helicopter
Degree of environmental sustainability	4 trees	3 trees	1 tree	2 trees	4 trees

What MASS learned during its first visit required us to go back to the very fundamentals of building. Many times, architects select materials much later in the design process after programming and massing studies, and it's often a process of browsing sample sets and catalogues to develop standard specifications. This was both undesirable and impossible for Ilima, and MASS focused only on materials that were locally available and could be utilized or improved, with a special emphasis on materials that, in their improvement, could benefit the culture of building within the region.

Most construction projects are far enough away from material extraction and refining that their workers have no first-hand knowledge of material pipelines or origins, never mind the environmental implications. Regenerative architecture should be more like the slow food movement, which connects to the origins of what we eat, in contrast to the processed fast foods in the aisles of our grocery stores.

We could have transported in a metal roof, but if it leaked, no one in the village would have had access to the materials to fix it. We found that other imported materials were relatively cheap to purchase, but their true cost would be borne out much later—poorly manufactured, they were not designed for longevity. MASS factored long-term impact, maintenance, and life cycles into every decision about materials, especially since the community becomes the ultimate caretakers of our design decisions. It's the reason Ilima's boards were sawn from lifake logs, its shingles hewn from tree rounds, its dyes made from bark, and rough textured leaves used as sandpaper. Everything we created had to be maintained, easily, by the village long after opening day.

Once we returned to our office in Rwanda, we began to delve into the properties, qualities, and possibilities of the earth, clay, wood, stone, and reed samples. In order to create earthen blocks, we had to determine which mixes resisted moisture. For our forested timber samples, we needed to know which woods were hard or soft, brittle or flexible, or lent themselves to splitting or cutting, and which species were more plentiful or rare. For our reeds, we had to verify which were accessible and plentiful, and which patterns of weaving or caning were possible. Very little at Ilima could be off-the-rack, including doors, windows, and chairs.

**Relearning How
to Build**

**by
Andrew Brose**

For MASS, relearning how to build at Ilima was about what seemed familiar and what could be innovative, but it was also about forging a deep connection with every tree stand, rock pile, and plant species within ten kilometers. In the end, it was a process of relearning how to be observant, respectful, and resourceful.

One of the most intriguing elements of the Congo Basin landscape were the termite mounds, often nearly thirty feet tall, eight of which populated the future site of the Ilima school. The digested soils that composed each mound were also excellent as a durable building material, which we first learned from our lead masons, Ekongo Modogo and Ziko Lokuli, and which we confirmed during our testing with the Arup materials lab.

The species *Macrotermes falciger* builds these expansive mounds, and in the process, imparts a binding saliva, adding to the soil's plasticity and strength. To utilize this resource responsibly, local builders harvest soil from abandoned mounds or from the outer layers of active mounds, ensuring the core colony remains undisturbed. This approach preserves the ecological role of termites, which includes soil aeration and nutrient cycling. As one of the primary building materials utilized by the community and given it is ecologically sound, plentiful, local, and low carbon, it was exciting to consider it as one of the building materials for the school.

We worked with Arup's material scientists to test all the sunbaked termite-digested earth blocks to understand the overall composition and strength, and also began testing additives that might improve the local recipe. Any additive would have to be easily sourced, and eventually we found that adding local palm oil, available from the Équateur Province plantations, increased the durability of the material by more than 20 percent by preventing surface deterioration. This certainly provided us with a solution for the Ilima school, but it also created a pathway for both homes and larger-scale buildings to use this adjusted recipe in Ilima village and further afield.

Collaborating with Termites

by Andrew Brose

Oil from palm nuts was
added to the bricks for
increased durability.

During our brief but immersive visit to the Équateur Province, we observed a range of furnishings that integrated weaving techniques, from woven chairs that community leaders carried to meetings, to intricate caning patterns such as the six-way and honeycomb associated with colonial furniture styles. In contrast, Ilima had almost no visible use of these techniques—raising questions for the MASS team about what styles and methods were appropriate and desirable for the Ilima school. Camile Abiyo, our head carpenter from Djolu, brought extensive experience in furniture-making, cabinetry, basic roof framing, and vannerie, a method of weaving and caning used in everything from chairs and doors to ceilings and floor mats. His expertise became integral to both the building and its furnishings.

The school's interior walls, which support the sweeping roof, were built from solid, sunbaked earth masonry. In contrast, the exterior walls needed to balance security with light and airflow. To achieve this, we worked with Camile to design a lightweight door frame on a pivot hinge that held a full-length, caned screen. These doors could be opened or closed to adjust for breeze or glare.

Once the school was well underway, the team focused on developing durable furniture that could withstand the normal wear and tear that any school endures, with a special emphasis on furniture that would be functional in the long-term. Poorly made or easily broken pieces, or any design strategy that didn't prioritize functionality, were not aligned with the long-term goals of self-sufficiency for this remote primary school. MASS pursued extensive prototyping and rigorous testing to guarantee resilience against heavy use and ensure that cost-efficiency and sustainability could be balanced for everything, from tables and chairs to fixtures and fittings crafted from nearby materials. The design created a lasting impact, offering students a safe, comfortable, and supportive learning environment, while also shrinking the carbon footprint of Ilima village's central hub.

**Caning &
Furnishing**

**by
Sierra Bainbridge
& Andrew Brose**

The conservation school agreements pursued by AWF during MASS's involvement in Ilima struck a balance between utilizing precious resources and preserving biodiverse ecologies. In this part of the equatorial rainforest, soil fertility declines after just two to three farming seasons, prompting communities to open new fields each year through slash-and-burn techniques—placing increasing pressure on the bonobo habitat. To slow this cycle, AWF adopted a two-pronged strategy aimed at supporting both ecological resilience and community well-being. First, they partnered with the community to test and de-risk regenerative agricultural practices; experimenting with new crop varieties, improving irrigation and tilling methods, and, crucially, organizing transport to Kinshasa to help farmers access markets. Second, they expanded educational access, creating economic pathways beyond subsistence farming and reinforcing the long-term value of conservation. In other regions, students who attend AWF schools have gone on to higher education, launched local businesses, or become rangers, guides, or conservation educators.

With these broader shifts in mind, the decision to build using local wood was a deliberate one. In a region where acres of forest would turn over to agriculture in the coming decades, using timber to construct a lasting piece of community infrastructure, one that might help stabilize settlement patterns and reduce deforestation, was not only justified, it was strategic.

The forest around Ilima is a dense canopy spread across a vast terrain with little topographical differentiation. Stories of people getting lost were common, while those who spent weeks deep within the maze of flora, such as hunters and woodcutters, had methods for retracing their steps. During the initial immersion, seven timber species were identified: bokoli (*Mammea africana*), boleko (*Ongokea gore*), bolenge (*Chrysophyllum africanum*), bolondo (*Milicia excelsa*), bolongo (*Symphonia globulifera*), lifake (*Entandrophragma utile*), and padauk (*Pterocarpus soyauxii*). After assessing these with the material engineers at Arup, two species stood out for their abundance, strength, and termite resistance: padauk, chosen for shingles and cladding, and bolondo (also known as iroko or African ebony), selected for columns, beams, and trusses. Both have relatively straight grain, good workability, and high durability—ideal for the tropical climate and available skill sets.

To reduce waste and simplify construction, the project was engineered around fourteen uniquely sized timber boards, each identified through a color-coded chart tied to drawings and construction details. The small unit size of padauk shingles (40 x 25 cm) allowed for a gently undulating roofline, otherwise impossible with rigid materials like corrugated zinc. Freshly cut, padauk glows a vivid red, standing out against the dark greens of the forest. The padauk shingles were created next to felled trees, leaving offcuts to fall to the forest floor and decompose naturally, returning nutrients to the soil. An attic stock of around five hundred shingles was prepared and stored for future roof repair.

Every Cut Considered

by Andrew Brose

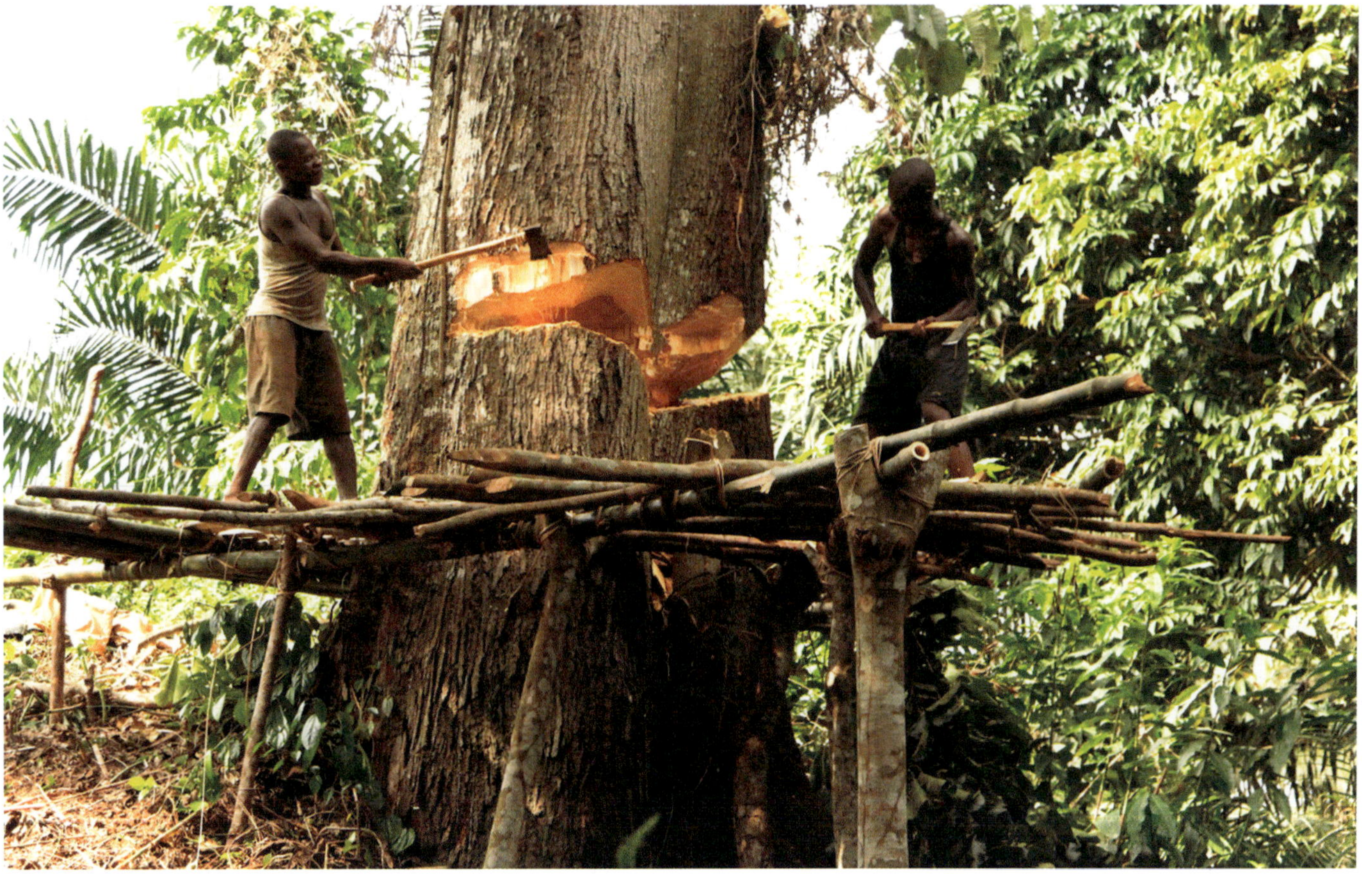

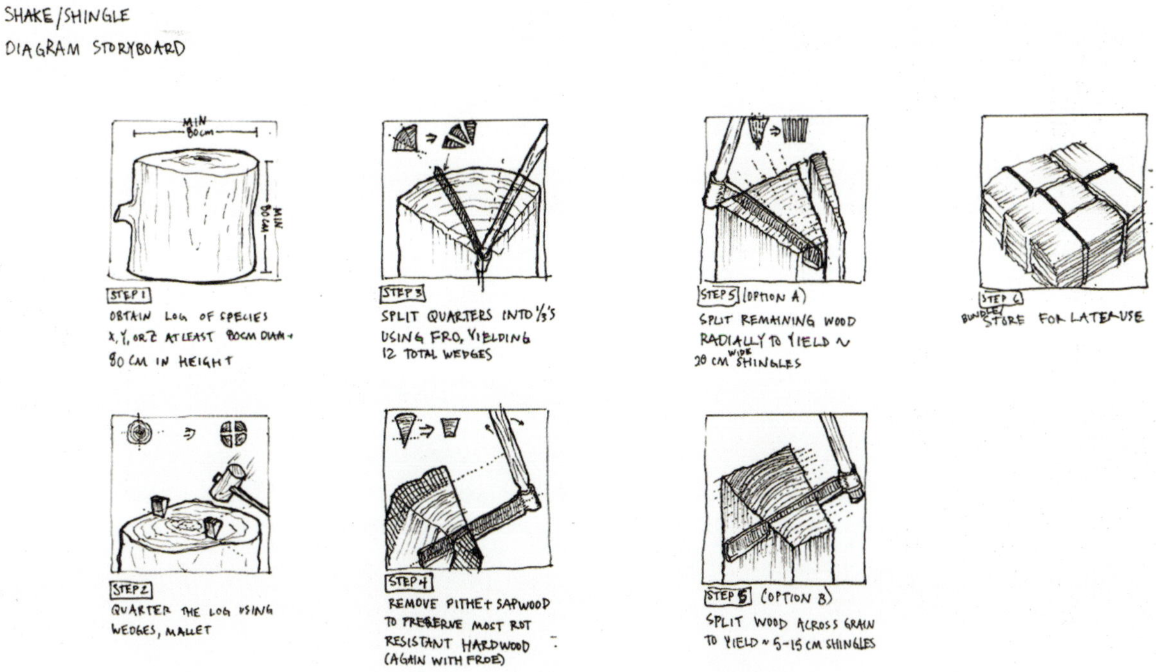

SHAKE/SHINGLE
DIAGRAM STORYBOARD
MIN 80cm
MIN 80cm
STEP 1
OBTAIN LOG OF SPECIES X, Y, OR Z AT LEAST 80CM DIAM + 80 CM IN HEIGHT
STEP 2
QUARTER THE LOG USING WEDGES, MALLET
STEP 3
SPLIT QUARTERS INTO 1/3'S USING FRO, YIELDING 12 TOTAL WEDGES
STEP 4
REMOVE PITH + SAPWOOD TO PRESERVE MOST ROT RESISTANT HARDWOOD (AGAIN WITH FROE)
STEP 5 (OPTION A)
SPLIT REMAINING WOOD RADIALLY TO YIELD ~ 20 CM WIDE SHINGLES
STEP 5 (OPTION B)
SPLIT WOOD ACROSS GRAIN TO YIELD ~ 5-15 CM SHINGLES
STEP 6
BUNDLE/STORE FOR LATER USE

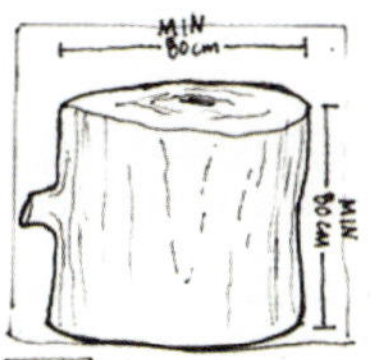

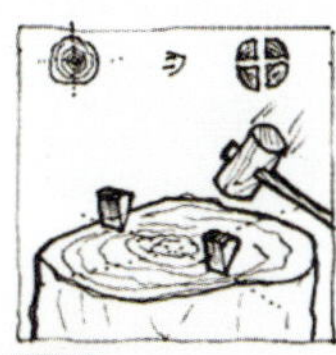

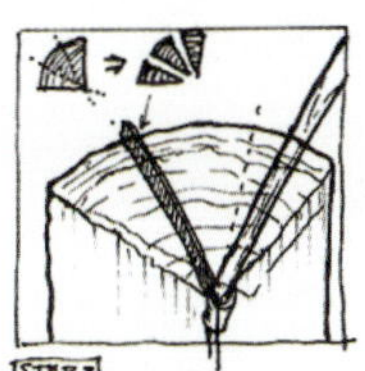

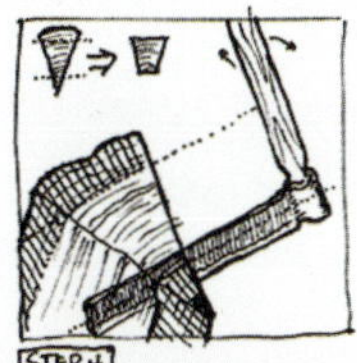

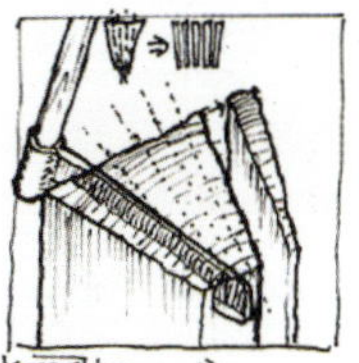

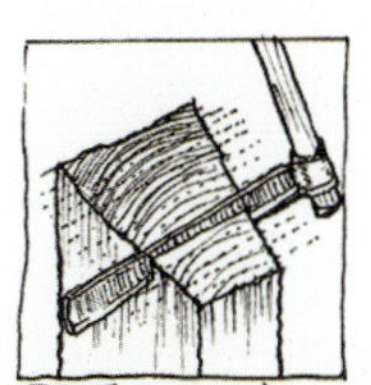

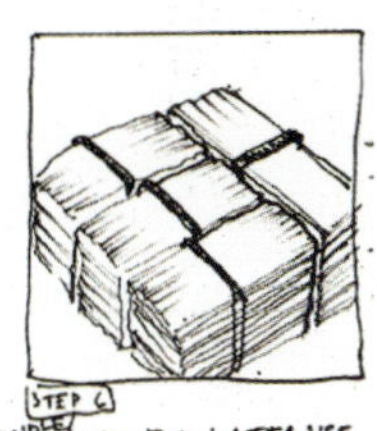

Congo Basin

The construction of the Ilima Primary School hinged on two essential crafts: masonry and carpentry. Yet neither trade was well established in the village, making training a foundational part of the project. MASS brought in skilled technicians from the nearby towns of Djolu, Mopono, and Boende to lead the effort. Once assembled on-site, the team immediately began producing bricks and boards, both of which required time to dry and cure before installation. This early phase also became a space for material innovation, as we explored new techniques grounded in local practice.

Skills training became a core pillar of community engagement at Ilima. Residents were invited to apprentice with master carpenters from Djolu, who agreed to travel for two days on foot to the building site to share techniques in timber sawing, structural framing, and eventually furniture construction and caning. Roofing, too, blended innovation with tradition, and project leaders researched suitable wood species for shingles, fabricated tools unavailable locally like the froe (an L-shaped implement used for splitting shingles), and worked alongside local craftspeople to build capacity directly on-site.

The project drew from the knowledge of carpenters, weavers, masons, and laborers, quite literally bringing the school out of the forest. The resulting building became a living expression of local knowledge, ecological stewardship, and collective purpose, revealing to us in new ways how meaningful infrastructure can emerge through shared investment.

Buildings only serve their purpose if they are embraced and sustained by the communities they're intended to serve. From the outset, MASS prioritized community participation, recruiting residents for frequent design meetings where they could share opinions and preferences. Local workers were trained in every stage of the building process, helping to ensure long-term stewardship and maintenance. MASS designed illustrated construction documents that were accessible to workers, many of whom could not read, which enabled between 160 and 170 people from Ilima and neighboring villages like Bolima and Lotulo to contribute to all aspects of the project, including the assembly of complex structural elements.

The school's construction also served as a platform for professional development. MASS mentored two Congolese architecture fellows on the Ilima project, placing them in leadership positions and immersing them in hands-on training with advanced, impact-driven construction techniques. Camile, a master carpenter from Djolu, also brought a deep background in cabinetry, furniture, and basic roof work to the site. However, assembling the nine-meter-long wooden trusses with precision nail patterns at every joint required multiple trials before reaching a reliable method. On-site furniture came together through small-scale wood framing, creatively woven fibers, and carefully crafted joinery that minimized reliance on imported hardware like nails. The building's distinctive curved roof and interlocking timber components pushed both design and construction teams to collaborate closely, exchanging sketches and ideas until they produced a hybrid drawing set that reflected both architectural intent and fabrication logic. The Ilima Primary School's mission, design, and construction were all grounded in the belief that conservation and community development is most feasible when we all are given the opportunity to develop in harmony with our surrounding natural environments.

Craft as a Living Legacy

by Andrew Brose

Natural systems and building systems came together in the diagrams used to help workers visualize the job.

THIS SYSTEM DOES NOT HAVE A DESIGN.
THIS HAS A DWG SET.

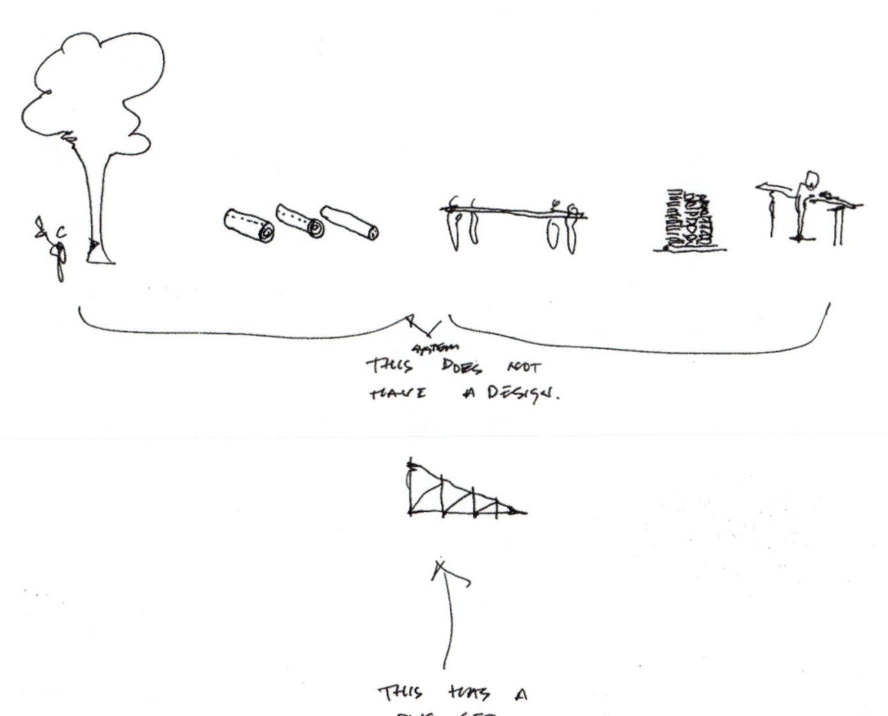

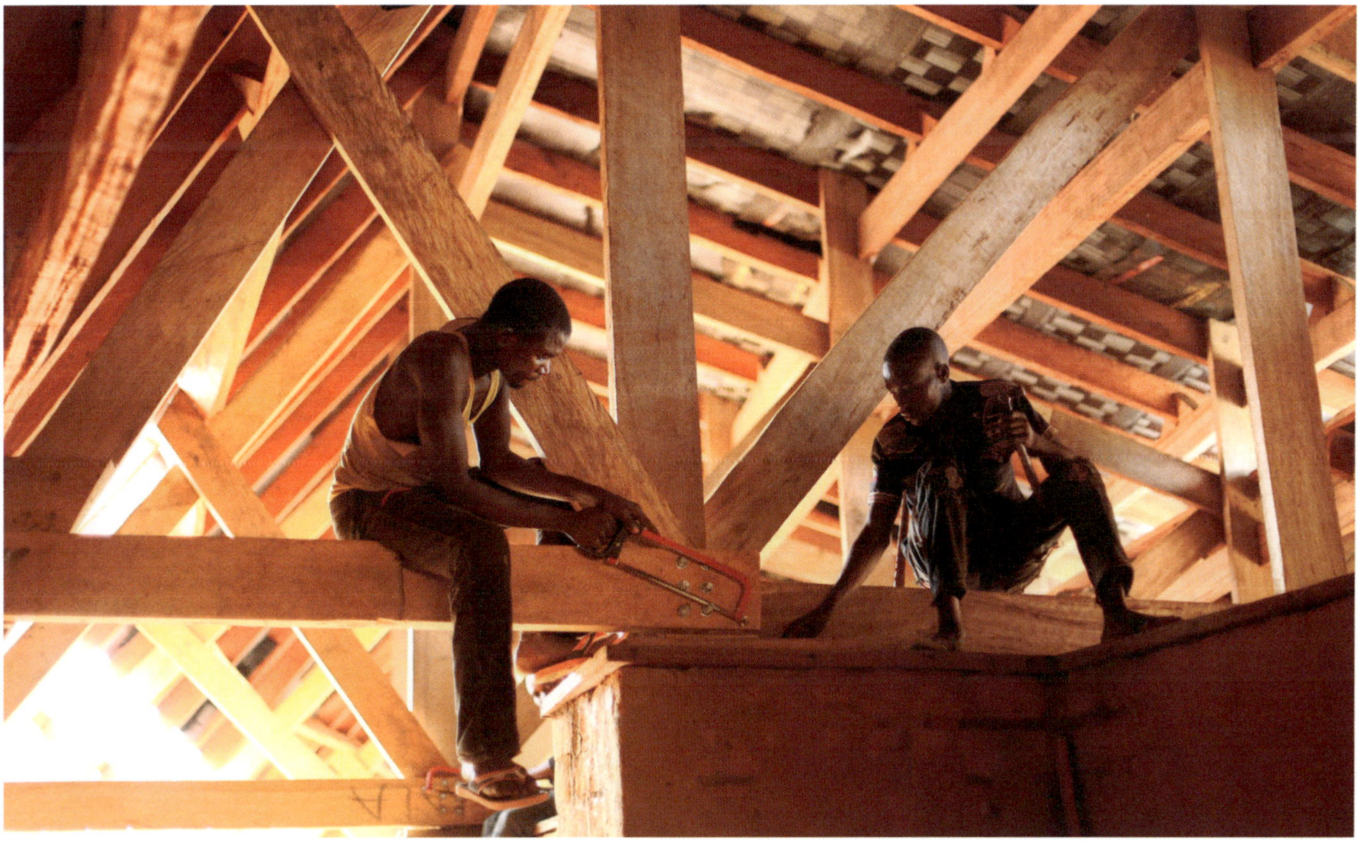

As a novice at this type of construction documentation, and because I was the only one recording the work on-site during most of the building process, I made the decision to list all the unique types of craft and made sure I captured video and images of each aspect. It even became a bit of a joke among the laborers not to do anything interesting without letting me first know about the work. I was in a unique position as a record keeper. Because of the remoteness of the site, the project had my undivided attention, and I could afford the time it took to traipse off into the woods when trees were felled and stones were quarried. I wasn't sure exactly what the end result would be for all the data I was collecting or video and photos I captured, so I made sure to focus on breadth, since there would be no going back once construction was finished.

It took some of the crew a while to warm up to my presence. They dismissed me as unimportant, since they couldn't imagine an outcome like the Ilima documentary, but I think they started to view their work with new eyes and enjoyed showing me Indigenous skills passed down from elders, like choosing different vines for weaving, selecting the right trees for construction, and knowing where to find different types of clay. In a place like Ilima, where there is just enough outside influence to realize the lack of options, I think this project, in addition to teaching new skills and ways to utilize materials, also built a sense of pride in local offerings.

**Framing
the Story**

**by
Rachel Brose**

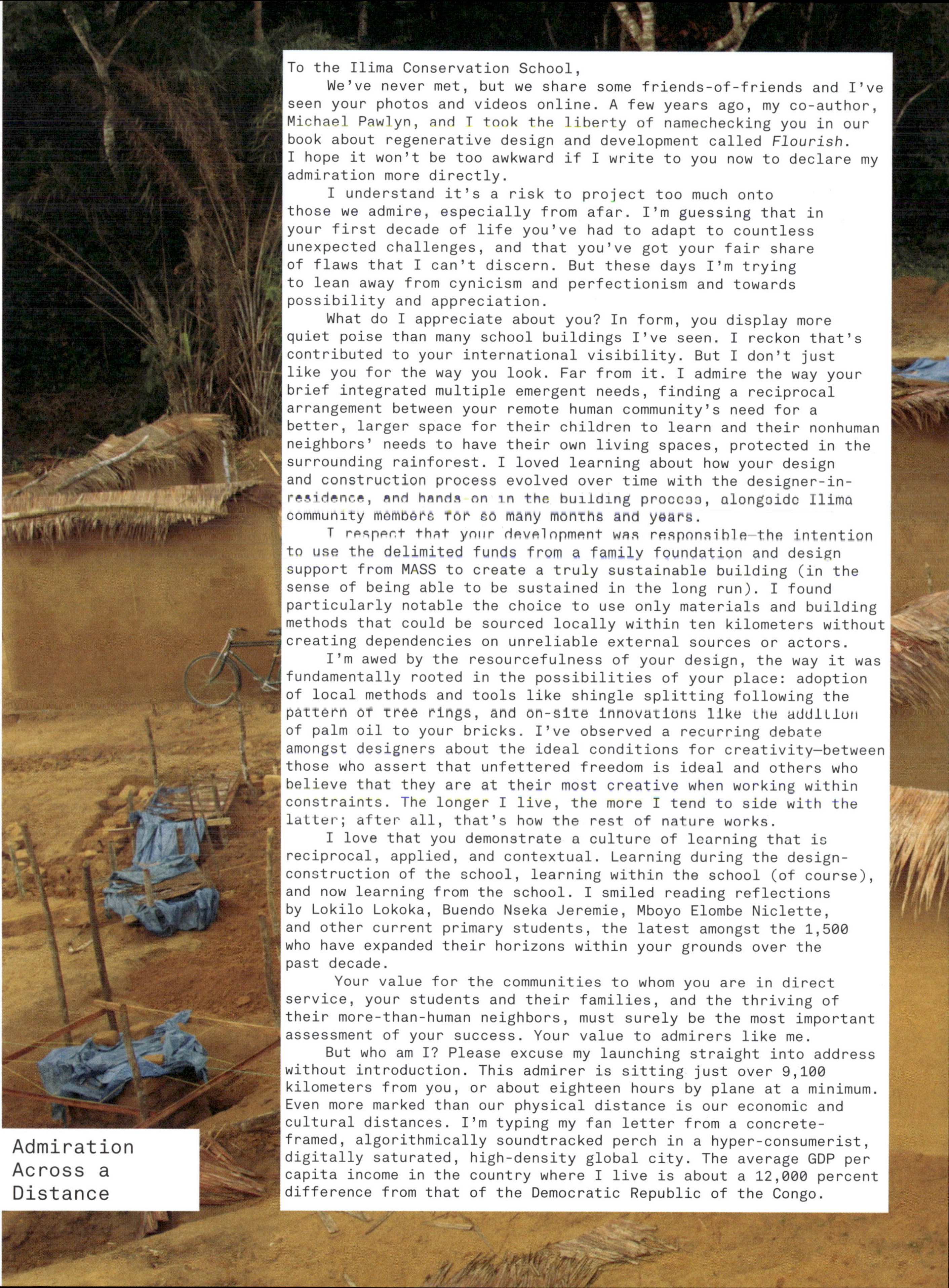

Admiration
Across a
Distance

To the Ilima Conservation School,

We've never met, but we share some friends-of-friends and I've seen your photos and videos online. A few years ago, my co-author, Michael Pawlyn, and I took the liberty of namechecking you in our book about regenerative design and development called *Flourish*. I hope it won't be too awkward if I write to you now to declare my admiration more directly.

I understand it's a risk to project too much onto those we admire, especially from afar. I'm guessing that in your first decade of life you've had to adapt to countless unexpected challenges, and that you've got your fair share of flaws that I can't discern. But these days I'm trying to lean away from cynicism and perfectionism and towards possibility and appreciation.

What do I appreciate about you? In form, you display more quiet poise than many school buildings I've seen. I reckon that's contributed to your international visibility. But I don't just like you for the way you look. Far from it. I admire the way your brief integrated multiple emergent needs, finding a reciprocal arrangement between your remote human community's need for a better, larger space for their children to learn and their nonhuman neighbors' needs to have their own living spaces, protected in the surrounding rainforest. I loved learning about how your design and construction process evolved over time with the designer-in-residence, and hands-on in the building process, alongside Ilima community members for so many months and years.

I respect that your development was responsible—the intention to use the delimited funds from a family foundation and design support from MASS to create a truly sustainable building (in the sense of being able to be sustained in the long run). I found particularly notable the choice to use only materials and building methods that could be sourced locally within ten kilometers without creating dependencies on unreliable external sources or actors.

I'm awed by the resourcefulness of your design, the way it was fundamentally rooted in the possibilities of your place: adoption of local methods and tools like shingle splitting following the pattern of tree rings, and on-site innovations like the addition of palm oil to your bricks. I've observed a recurring debate amongst designers about the ideal conditions for creativity—between those who assert that unfettered freedom is ideal and others who believe that they are at their most creative when working within constraints. The longer I live, the more I tend to side with the latter; after all, that's how the rest of nature works.

I love that you demonstrate a culture of learning that is reciprocal, applied, and contextual. Learning during the design-construction of the school, learning within the school (of course), and now learning from the school. I smiled reading reflections by Lokilo Lokoka, Buendo Nseka Jeremie, Mboyo Elombe Niclette, and other current primary students, the latest amongst the 1,500 who have expanded their horizons within your grounds over the past decade.

Your value for the communities to whom you are in direct service, your students and their families, and the thriving of their more-than-human neighbors, must surely be the most important assessment of your success. Your value to admirers like me.

But who am I? Please excuse my launching straight into address without introduction. This admirer is sitting just over 9,100 kilometers from you, or about eighteen hours by plane at a minimum. Even more marked than our physical distance is our economic and cultural distances. I'm typing my fan letter from a concrete-framed, algorithmically soundtracked perch in a hyper-consumerist, digitally saturated, high-density global city. The average GDP per capita income in the country where I live is about a 12,000 percent difference from that of the Democratic Republic of the Congo.

I imagine that many of your other admirers may make their living through the hands-on collective construction of ethically-funded buildings using local materials. I, on the other hand, spend much of my day moving bits around on a screen, or talking into a camera, to deliver services like "strategic organizational transformation" and "critical cultural diplomacy."

Viewed from this perspective, I value another aspect in addition to those already praised. This is: I appreciate the way in which you make tangible ideas that are too often—at least by the people in my circle, in my context—diminished through abstraction. Do you know the kinds of ideas I'm talking about? Right livelihoods. Interspecies compacts. Designing as nature.

Do you know the kind of people and circles I'm talking about? Davos-whisperers wielding elegant diagrams, LinkedIn hawkers of white-label ubuntu inspo, Biennale curators of sci-fi provocations. Highly visible, well-intentioned people who are really excited about systems change, but who might struggle to find north in a new landscape, or to keep the plant on their desk alive. Those kinds of people are also my friends, and also—sometimes—include the face in my mirror.

My friends are A-grade theorists and five-figure keynote-givers. But has this done much good aside from making us feel better about ourselves? I mean: Look at where we are. The accumulated actions of societies like the ones I grew up in and now live in have decimated many of the natural systems that support the Earth's thriving, and concentrated power in the clenched fists of a few, insatiable men. If, in the face of this storm, the wealthy world's credentialed classes continue to deal in abstractions, pieties and fantasies, then maybe we deserve what's coming for us.

So, I want to tell all my friends about you, because you offer us an example of what is possible practically, not speculatively. Aspiring community-clients, funders, and designers around the world can give thanks to your designers and funders for documenting the co-creative processes that brought your structure into being in a way that can inspire us and, more importantly, teach us.

The modest specificity of what you and your community in Ilima have achieved might just rescue us from our obsession with "scaling up." Your example might help guide us to seek a new reciprocity between globalized flows of knowledge and localized flows of materials. You might remind us that protecting and learning with a diversity of human cultures is key to conserving and restoring the diversity of the rest of the web of life, and that this cannot take place generically, but in whatever particular place we find ourselves.

All of this to say: Thank you for your role as a beacon for geographically rooted, culturally specific, mutual thriving. You're not a concept. You're not an image. You're not a fungible asset. You're a living thing.

We likely won't ever meet each other face-to-face, but I am hopeful that I may yet meet your siblings, cousins, and children as they take shape in the many places and communities around the world that are daring to commit themselves to integrated thriving and embodied care.

With gratitude and respect,
Sarah Mineko Ichioka

Singapore
March 2025

Sarah Mineko Ichioka is an urbanist, strategist, curator, and writer. She leads Desire Lines, a strategic consultancy for environmental, cultural, and social-impact initiatives and organizations.

A decade ago, I had never heard the term "embodied carbon." At no stage in my education, training, and licensure as a Canadian architect had these two words appeared. As a student, and a member of the post-OPEC crisis generation, my attention had been focused solely on how to best reduce the emissions associated with the operations of a building. But then I moved to Rwanda, a rapidly developing, landlocked nation with few mineral resources, an abundance of labor, and an 18 percent import tax, the set of constraints that had created MASS. Out of necessity, every design decision we made sought to minimize imported materials and maximize domestic labor. The financial inversion of parts and labor in Rwanda required working side by side with our structural and geotechnical engineers to find pathways to limit cement, steel, and glass, all materials that come primarily from external sources, and expand the roles of manual construction and craft. In order to build, we first asked, "What materials are regionally abundant?" and, "Who can we work with to build them?" This line of questioning results in an architecture in and of its place, one that routes the investments in building into an investment in community.

I joined MASS at a moment of inflection in the practice. We were completing a series of projects that had brought methods honed in Rwanda to other parts of the world, notably the Cholera Treatment Centre in Haiti and Ilima in the Democratic Republic of the Congo, and were about to embark on a series of institutional projects that would test our capacity to push this approach at ever-larger scales. Our focus on the social impacts of these decisions also began to broaden. Through a collaboration with researchers at MIT, we began to take a deeper dive into the ecological impacts of our projects and gained our first glimpse at the emissions associated with the excavation, harvesting, processing, transportation, and construction of our buildings. We learned that the social and environmental impacts of our decisions completely overlapped—that the building's carbon footprint had a direct relationship with the human handprint of its making. Heavily processed, carbon-intensive materials, primarily metals and plastics, carried significant social and ecological impacts. Conversely, the lowest carbon materials in our projects, locally quarried stone and site-made compressed earth blocks, also meant that the budgets of construction were directed into as many local pockets as possible.

Notably, we learned that the Ilima Primary School had one twenty-eighth of the upfront embodied carbon footprint of the global average primary school. This remote school, hewn from the Congolese forest surrounding it, totally destabilized my understanding of architecture. What had I been doing? What were the implications of my decisions? To better understand my impacts, I returned to the summer home recently designed for my in-laws, a building also located in a forest and built of wood, and taught myself how to perform a life cycle assessment. I discovered that the construction of the building emitted ninety-two tons of carbon, the equivalent of ninety-two years of driving a car. I discovered that over half of that was attributable to two materials made from oil—two materials totally absent in Ilima—extruded polystyrene insulation and asphalt shingle. I realized that I'd been practicing with an enormous, oil-stained blind spot.

Harvesting Architecture from the Site

by Kelly Alvarez Doran

Our agency as architects sits almost
entirely in what we build with, where we
source it from, and who we build with. While
we have some influence over how buildings
are operated and maintained, our ability to
control and mitigate ultimately stops the
moment a building is occupied. It is through
drawings and specifications, and the billions
of dollars they direct every year, that we
can most effectively address the social,
environmental, and political challenges we
face. This reality overlaps with the life
cycle emissions of a building: In many
parts of the world, the embodied emissions
of constructing and maintaining a building
will eclipse the emissions associated with a
lifetime of its operations. It is therefore
imperative that we question what we're
building with, interrogate the methods we're
currently using, and work together to find
lower-carbon alternatives. Are we sourcing
our materials from parts of the world with
questionable labor practices or oppressive
regimes, or working with producers and
suppliers with whom we can see firsthand the
impacts of decision-making?

We brought this new understanding to
RICA. From the outset, we attempted to
harvest a built project from the site, one
that made the highest and best use of its
resources and one that would direct the
project's incredible investment into pockets
across Rwanda. Every design decision made
by our multidisciplinary team was grounded
in material sufficiency, passive design, and
cost-effective construction. The project
that employed thousands, designed and built
through COVID, and is now recognized with
multiple international awards, offers a
glimpse at what a post-petroleum architecture
might just look like.

In 2020, I reached out to the University
of Toronto to offer students the lessons I'd
learned in Rwanda, and to find ways to have
them translate to the Canadian context. Over
the past five years the Ha/f Studio has been
engaging practitioners across Canada, the
United States, and Europe through case studies
of buildings. The studio's findings have led
to policy work with the City of Toronto,
resulting in North America's first embodied
carbon caps, to the formation of a company,
to research and guidance with the Government
of Canada, and to the training of hundreds of
fellow architects across Canada and the UK.
Ha/f is helping to bring the lessons of Ilima
and RICA to projects and practitioners around
the world.

Kelly Alvarez Doran
is co-founder of
Ha/f Climate Design.
Previously, he was a
principal in MASS's
Africa Studio.

In 2025, the pace at which the world is
facing global challenges is accelerating
at an unprecedented rate. Technological
advancements, particularly the development
of large language models and artificial
intelligence, are disrupting societies at
every level. Simultaneously, the impacts of
climate change and biodiversity loss are
becoming increasingly severe and, in many
cases, irreversible. The world is in urgent
need of innovative solutions and a renewed
vision to navigate the uncertain future ahead.

Central Africa is no exception to these
challenges, as the past fifty years or more
have demonstrated. The region has endured
ongoing conflicts, high and rising—though
unevenly distributed—population densities,
and pressing issues at the intersection of
urban development, biodiversity conservation,
security, and agricultural expansion.

Now more than ever, biodiversity remains
one of our most powerful assets in the
fight against a rapidly changing climate.
Yet, biodiversity loss is accelerating at
an alarming rate. While land scarcity is a
significant factor, it is not the only one.
A widespread belief—sometimes justified—is
that biodiversity conservation and economic
development are in direct conflict. Many argue
that developing nations should not be expected
to slow their progress to preserve the
environment, particularly when much of
the world's environmental degradation has
stemmed from the industrialization of the
Global North.

However, this perceived competition
between development and conservation is
not inevitable. New approaches to holistic
development offer a unique opportunity to be
explored and implemented—before the costs of
reversing the damage become too high or before
irreversible harm is done.

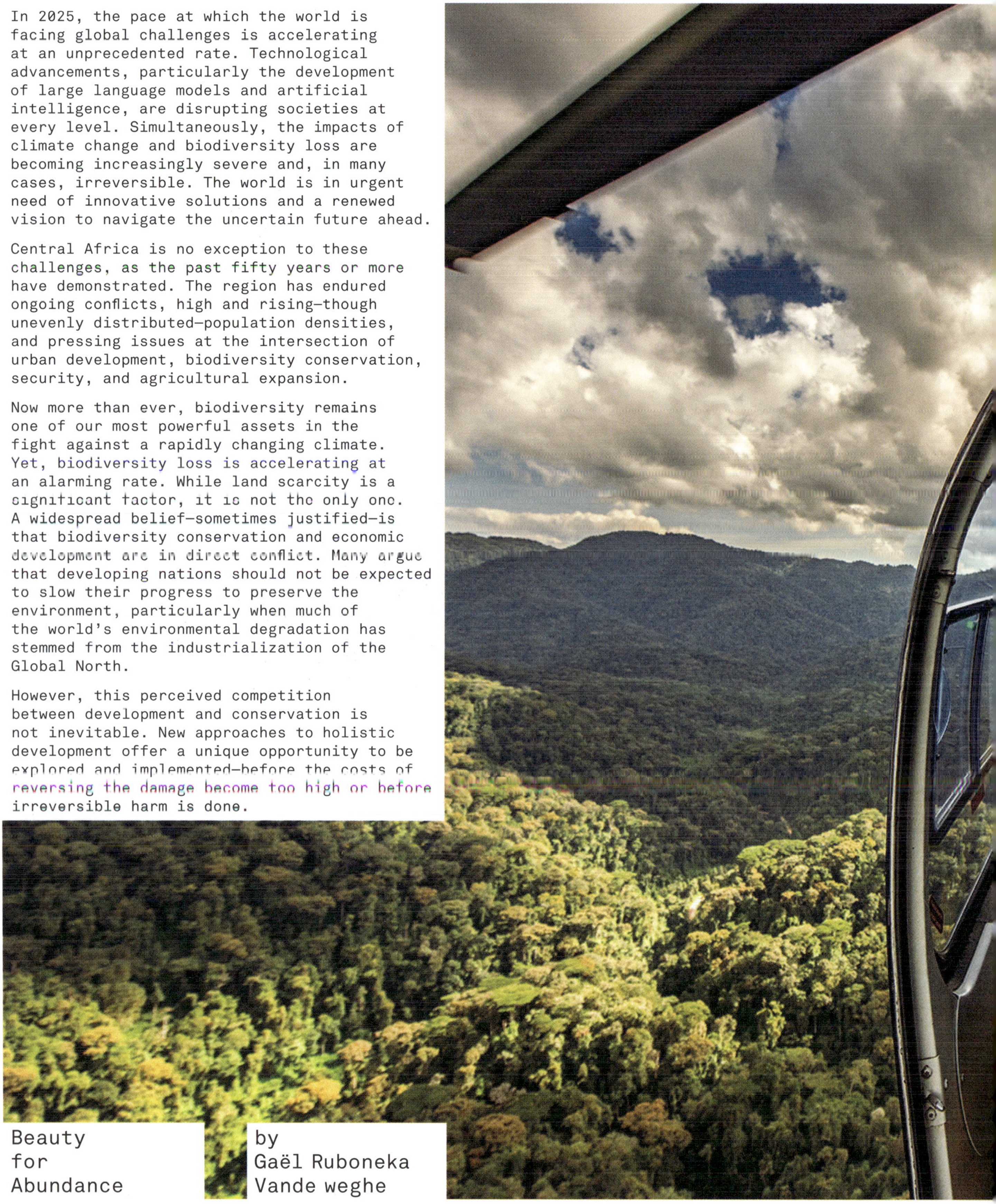

Beauty   by
for   Gaël Ruboneka
Abundance   Vande weghe

One Health is a Human and Ecological Framework
One Health is a multidisciplinary approach recognizing the deep interconnections between human health, animal populations, and ecosystems. In Central Africa, where zoonotic diseases such as Ebola and emerging viruses pose significant threats, strengthening this framework is imperative. Deforestation, climate change, and urban sprawl have increased human-wildlife interactions, heightening health risks. Integrated policies that consider biodiversity conservation, sustainable agriculture, and urban planning are essential for disease prevention and long-term resilience. The inclusion of anti-deforestation policies, rewilding, and environmental education would greatly improve human-wildlife interactions and limit the negative effects of uncontrolled extractive practices.

Biodiversity plays a fundamental role in urban resilience, offering ecosystem services such as air purification, water filtration, and climate regulation. In many Central African cities, rapid and often unplanned urbanization threatens these natural benefits. Architectural solutions that incorporate green spaces, living walls, and nature-based infrastructure can mitigate these effects while enhancing public health and social well-being. For example, designing cities that accommodate wetlands rather than draining them can reduce flood risks while preserving vital habitats.

Cultural integration and environmental education play a crucial role in fostering acceptance of a closer relationship with nature, particularly in contexts where societal disruption, urbanization, and unsustainable agriculture have distanced people from their natural surroundings. In many cases, nature is perceived as hostile, leading to excessive removal and degradation of ecosystems. The rapid shift toward imported models of modernity, without the inclusion of traditional knowledge and cultural practices, has contributed to a disconnect from nature. This disruption has created a context in which human development is often at odds with ecological sustainability, rather than in harmony with it. As a result, environmental literacy remains very low.

Beauty for Abundance

Historically, African architecture has harmonized with nature, utilizing locally available materials and climate-responsive designs. Contemporary architectural trends in Central Africa can revive these principles while integrating modern technology. Biophilic design, which seeks to reconnect people with nature, presents an opportunity to create spaces that are not only functional but also aesthetically enriching. By drawing inspiration from traditional dwellings—such as the elevated houses of the Congo Basin or the adobe structures of the Sahel—architects can design sustainable buildings that minimize environmental impact while maintaining cultural identity.

The beauty of nature can be the medium through which empathy towards nature becomes more widespread, allowing natural innovation and ecological systems to be integrated into form and function—resulting in unique innovations and new designs that will be more easily communicated and accepted by the communities. Beauty in design also goes beyond aesthetics; it fosters well-being, resilience, and a sense of belonging. Architecture that incorporates biodiversity and ecological balance creates environments where people can thrive physically and psychologically.

Urban areas designed with abundant green spaces, natural light, and organic forms contribute to a sense of harmony between humans and their surroundings. Beauty inspired by the infinite possible inspirations provided by nature in all its glory can provide a balance for sustainability and can help redefine development paradigms, showing that progress does not have to come at the expense of nature.

Hope in Innovation—A Vision for the Future

Despite the uncertainties facing Central Africa, innovative approaches in One Health, biodiversity conservation, and architecture offer tremendous opportunities. Urban planners, businesses, and policymakers can work together to co-create green cities, foster sustainable housing solutions, and ensure that human health is intrinsically linked to environmental well-being. Furthermore, investing in community-based conservation and regenerative agriculture will create economic opportunities while preserving the region's rich natural heritage, which will be embedded in the created social fabric.

Where Should We Go from Here?

A shift toward holistic, nature-based solutions is not only possible but necessary. The integration of biodiversity into urban planning, the recognition of Indigenous knowledge in development strategies, and the use of sustainable materials in architecture provide opportunities to reshape the future. By embracing ecological and cultural richness as assets rather than obstacles, Central Africa can lead the way in redefining progress for a more resilient world. The beauty of nature's tapestry and its integration in functioning societies can be the catalyst towards a more abundant world that has shifted away from unsustainable and destructive practices. This beauty can be one of the important languages towards much higher rates of acceptance of these renewed ideas. They are already largely used by the arts and by tourism. They now need to be integrated into innovation, collaboration, societies, and individual lifestyles.

—Gaël R. Vande weghe

Gaël Ruboneka Vande weghe, who grew up in Rwanda, is a photographer and artist.

Savannah Woodland

Savannah
Woodland   RICA

The Rwanda Institute for Conservation Agriculture (RICA) is a working landscape, an ecological restoration effort, and an educational model rolled into one. Located on a 3,400-acre peninsula in Rwanda's Bugesera District, the campus was designed to address a complex and urgent question: How can we feed a growing population while restoring, rather than depleting, the ecosystems on which food production depends?

Over the last fifty years Rwanda has become the most densely populated country in sub-Saharan Africa, with over 591 people per square kilometer. As the population continues to grow—projected to double by 2050—the demands on land, food production, and ecological stability will intensify dramatically.

Today, nearly every arable acre not protected or infertile has already been put into agricultural use. But even with this full utilization, Rwanda still imports food. The government has set an ambitious goal: to achieve food independence within a generation. To do this, agricultural productivity must double or even triple, even as the land suffers from erosion, nutrient depletion, and climate volatility.

What makes this challenge even more urgent is that food production cannot be isolated from environmental health. Future agriculture must depend on thriving ecosystems that support pollination, water regulation, pest control, and biodiversity. Warmer temperatures have expanded the habitats of vector-borne disease carriers such as mosquitoes, and land conversion has caused natural predators of these insects to migrate or become extinct.

RICA's campus is surrounded by one of the last remaining patches of savannah woodland outside Rwanda's national parks. These woodlands are now protected—and integrated into the design of the school itself. Ecological corridors link the woodlands to nearby wetlands, allowing for the movement of animals, insects, and water. The restored ecosystem supports soil regeneration, carbon sequestration, and climate resilience, while also directly improving agricultural yields. At RICA, biodiversity is not adjacent to agriculture—it supports it.

RICA's mission is not only to grow food, but to grow the next generation of agricultural leaders. The curriculum is experiential, centered around cooperative learning and entrepreneurship. Students live in housing that is deeply tied to their learning. First-year students are assigned to on-site smallholder farms in cohorts of up to twenty-one students, managing a two-acre plot and building community through shared work. Upper-year housing supports informal learning, peer mentorship, and collaborative experimentation. Classrooms are placed adjacent to test plots, irrigation pivots, and livestock zones—turning every building into a living laboratory. Students learn not only to cultivate, but to manage, innovate, and lead.

The design of the campus mirrors this pedagogical model. The buildings are constructed using low-carbon materials such as timber, stone, and compressed earth blocks. Everything, down to the clay tiles fired with coffee husks, is intended to be replicable and regenerative, modeling the type of innovation expected of the students who attend the university.

Community engagement and national impact were core from the start. Construction involved over 1,200 workers, 90 percent of whom came from the surrounding Bugesera District. Materials were sourced locally, workforce training was embedded into the process, and the economic benefits of the project were kept within the region.

RICA is more than a campus. It is a proof of concept, a demonstration that sustainable agriculture, ecological conservation, and educational excellence can coexist—and in fact, reinforce one another.

Creating an Unprecedented Campus for Agricultural Education

Land use changes have transformed Rwanda
in the last fifty years, with the
majority of native forest and grasslands
converted to agricultural production.

1990

2017

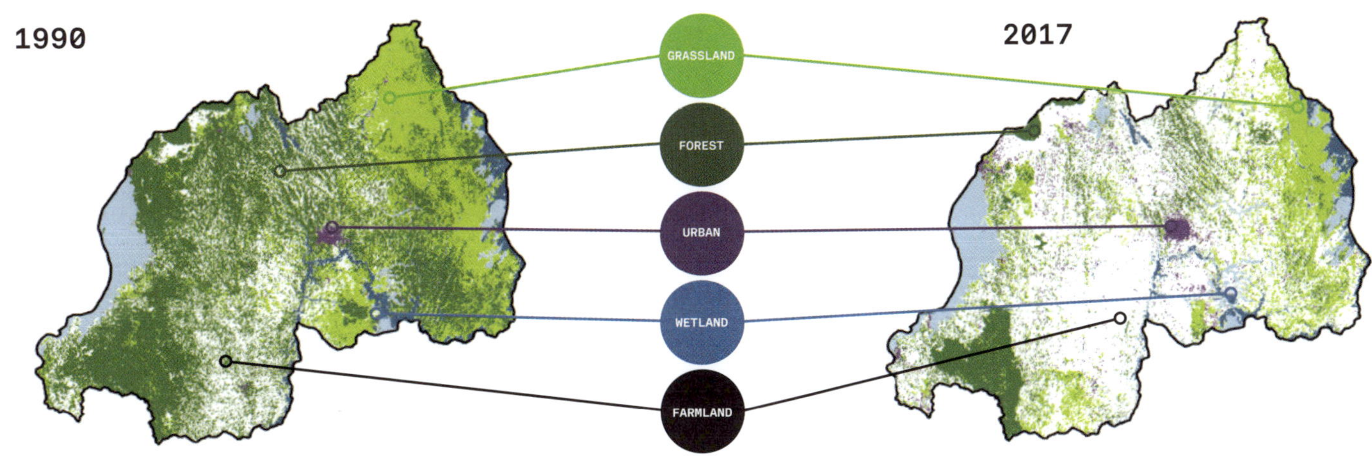

Land area

26,338 sq. km total,
bordering Burundi (315 km),
Democratic Republic of the Congo (221 km),
Tanzania (222 km),
and Uganda (172 km)

Mean elevation

1,598 m

Population total

13,623,302

Languages

* Kinyarwanda (official,
  universal Bantu vernacular) 93.2%
* French (official) <0.1%
* English (official) <0.1%
* Swahili/Kiswahili (official,
  used in commercial centers) <0.1%

The planting approach for RICA was designed
with the intention of fostering the benefits of
One Health by encouraging the expansion of the
native food web. Biodiversity loss within the region
of Bugesera has been extensive, with the majority
of the landscape having been transformed into
monoculture agriculture and non-native species.
The presence of an intact woodland savannah on
the site offered a jumping-off point to begin to
restore biodiversity through its protection
and served as a source for plant propagation.
The diversity of species that are native to this
region is expansive and their interconnection
helps to strengthen the health of the land as well
as increase the agricultural output of the fields.

Species Collection and Propagation

Savannah Woodland

RICA, as a campus and as a curriculum, is built to address national projections for more people, less growing land per farmer, climate volatility, and competing environmental interests by 2050. Its governing strategy, One Health, holds that human, ecological, and animal health are interconnected, not categorically separate interests. At RICA, and in all of our projects that utilize One Health, every decision is considered in light of how it will influence other pieces of the larger picture. It's also the basis of RICA's curriculum, designed by MASS to coordinate with the campus design itself, creating a unique relationship between us, the school, and graduates who go on to utilize One Health principles in their agricultural work.

RICA's stakeholders wanted to grow more food, while improving the surrounding environments of forest and wetland. The One Health curriculum at RICA demonstrates how agriculture is implemented at different scales. Instructors cover a range of topics, from conservation biology to agricultural economics, including disease prevention as a critical aspect of maintaining healthy, resilient systems. In their first year, RICA's students imagine themselves in 2050 and learn to live on a farm that produces enough food to feed themselves and to sell, as well. In their second year, students learn how to implement processes that add value to their operation, for example, making yogurt and sauces. In the third year, students work together to learn about larger capital expenses and agricultural efficiencies, and spend six months in a practical internship that serves as a capstone experience.

In all its design decisions, MASS began with carbon positive and One Health concepts that could demonstrate pedagogical concepts on-site. We engineered bioswales planted with erosion-preventing native grasses that filter runoff instead of using concrete-lined drainage channels. The solar field that powers RICA is lined with flora that provide livestock a pasture. These and other decisions put One Health into action and provide RICA with the foundation it needs to influence regional sustainable growth over the next thirty years—graduating classes of farmers and entrepreneurs who can improve Rwanda's human, ecological, and animal health while growing a prosperous economy.

**RICA's
One Health
Curriculum as
Connective
Tissue**

by

Jessi Flynn

Healthy wetlands filter the nation's water, while native vegetation replenishes the nutrient-rich soil.

1   Healthy Ecosystem

Across the country, land is being cleared to make room for agriculture and to acquire firewood.

1   Clearing
2   Deforestation

Seasonal wetlands are taken over for grazing and crops, this conversion increasing with longer dry seasons and extended droughts. Erosion pollutes waterways and strips away the productivity of the land.

1   Clearing
2   Deforestation
3   Topsoil Erosion
4   Papyrus Removal

A conversation about creating the world's first climate-positive university that fosters food independence and seeks the balance between human, ecological, and animal health.

AL   Before RICA, I think Ilima is our clearest example of context-driven design, trying to source as much as possible in close proximity to the site. The earth blocks, the timber for the roof structure, and even the roof shingles made out of hardwood, all were sourced within a few miles. When we looked at the impact report, seeing that we minimized the environmental impact by sourcing 99 percent of materials from within ten miles was a really clear lesson in needing to think about sourcing and our supply chain. But also, these choices amplified the project's economic impact through the relatively large investment to build a building within the community.

KAD   At RICA we had the opportunity to push the processes of Ilima to an altogether different scale, working across a much larger site and building sixty-nine buildings. We asked how we could go further than just thinking locally, and reflect the mission of the school in the way we harvested materials for the site. Those questions set the tone for the ambition of the project from the beginning. We did extensive research into the site and the region, but things all changed when we hired Samuel Nshutiyayesu, an ecologist, to document the biodiversity on the site.

AL   Sam's research uncovered that this was the biggest savannah woodland outside Akagera National Park and was home to some rare wildlife. We saw this not just as a constraint, but as a massive ecological asset—reconnecting the savannah woodland forest to the papyrus-lined edge of the lake. We had to think about an approach that would balance agricultural productivity with the conservation of these ecological systems. This was the foundation for a One Health approach—valuing the interdependence of ecological, animal, and human health.

Investigating
the Forensics
of the Site

SB   Up to this point, when Sam shared the history of the site, we had considered building within the forested area and nestling the building within it. It became clearer that if we were going to take a One Health approach, siting the buildings and locating the entire curriculum for this campus had to value and prioritize an intact ecology. We shared with the team the idea of patch dynamics, how larger tracts of land—unbroken by roads or development, with intact systems of water flow and animal movements—had to be preserved and maintained. And not just for the sake of it. We understood from prior projects and studies coming out continually that our future food security relies on proximity to health ecology.

AL   To me, vernacular intelligence means asking: What was here one hundred years ago, and how can that inform what and how we build today? It's about recognizing the embedded wisdom in place, people, and material culture. At RICA, that meant designing with the land and not against it—understanding how traditional practices and ecological systems can inform future resilience. Climate resilience, in this context, comes from ecological integration—from restoring biodiversity, storing carbon in the soil, managing water through natural systems, and cooling environments through vegetation. Nature already holds many of the solutions to the climate crisis. We just need to listen, observe, and design accordingly.

KAD   We're completely off grid. RICA wanted energy autonomy because of the unreliability of the existing grid. But beyond that, the reality of the cost of bringing power to the site was pretty prohibitive. Rwanda's power is very carbon intensive. Its electrical grid is powered largely by heavy fuel oil and methane. As a result, the grid intensity of electricity in Rwanda is incredibly high. So the opportunity to go fully renewable and fully off-site was significant.

AL   Here, infrastructure isn't an afterthought. It's embedded into the different project systems, from renewable energy systems to closed-loop water cycles, designed for resilience. The dry conditions at RICA reflect much of East Africa's climate, making water conservation and reuse essential. These set precedents for similar climates and contexts—showing how infrastructure can be designed not just to withstand environmental pressures, but to work in harmony with local ecosystems.

CH   Infrastructure at RICA is as much about creating capacity for its operations as it is about conserving resources—and protecting the lake for their drinking water, which then forced us to confront waste management from the beginning of the process. That feeds into the idea of the One Health master plan, where the treatment of wastewater and rainwater is always seen in light of the lake, working with bioswales and gravity to manage flows and also creating a methodology for RICA's students to see in action and then take with them when they leave the campus.

AR   The concepts of One Health really drove the overall site design and where programs were located. But we also wanted these principles and the ethos of the school and conservation to drive the building design. The buildings had to be highly functional, meeting the needs of the experiential curriculum, but also create spaces of comfort for the students and faculty who spend large portions of their day outside. The lessons from Ilima applied here as well, where we looked at opportunities to use local materials not only to serve these needs, but also to create jobs and maximize the value of this investment in the community.

AL   The original contractor that had been hired ran into financial challenges. Once again we were faced with a challenge where delegating responsibility means a loss of agency over the impact. We took over as the general contractor and hired almost all of their staff who had lost their jobs over the subsequent two weeks. That move wasn't just about finishing the campus—it was about sticking to the mission. It not only ensured the continuity of the project during an unprecedented crisis, but also created the conditions for RICA to deliver on its mission: training a new generation of leaders in conservation agriculture.

AR   We had an unusual level of control over the project because the Howard G. Buffett Foundation provided us with the grant to not only design but to see the project built. We had to navigate all of the contracting, and in this unusual situation decided to take on all of the risk of building the project. This afforded us the ability to control the methods of construction and deploy numerous more innovative approaches that would have been hard to incorporate in other circumstances. And it allowed us to integrate the principles of impact, from the scale of the site and ecosystem design down to the scale of buildings and landscapes, and even the furniture.

JPSU   When the project opened, we had more than one hundred Rwandan architects visit in a short period. Everybody was like, "Wow, we didn't think that this was possible." It was pretty eye-opening for everybody, especially those in the industry, to see that it is possible to do something that is not usual in this market.

CH   There are a few things that are really different about this project. I remember a government official was on the RICA advisory board when we designed it and he was skeptical of using earth as the main material and as a finish on the interior rooms. When I gave him

the first tour of the first building, he was convinced. When he walked in the space there was an immediate temperature adjustment, so you could really appreciate the thick thermal mass of the earth keeping the interiors cool and comfortable. And he looked back at the team and he gave us a little grin.

AL   When President Kagame toured the campus during the main opening and saw the use of timber and earth at scale, he reportedly called the Ministry of Infrastructure immediately, encouraging them to come to the site and consider how this approach could be implemented elsewhere. That same afternoon, the ministry's team arrived to study our application of these natural materials. The moment catalyzed a shift in perception, offering a tangible example of what's possible. Since then, we've seen a ripple effect: Lodges and homes are now being designed with rammed earth and timber structures, signaling a growing aspiration toward natural materials and regenerative design, reducing energy consumption and improving self-sufficiency.

JPSU   As somebody who's been trained in Rwanda—I was in the first class of architects in 2009—looking at this project is an opportunity for us to rethink architecture and how we teach it. For the last decade there has been a proliferation of glass-clad, mechanically cooled buildings that appear like what you see in other cities but are totally misaligned with our climate. RICA set an example that something can be modern and progressive, while still working with local materials and traditional craft.

AL   RICA is ambitious, yes. It's a design born from constraint, shaped by place, and led by purpose. It combines regenerative materials, local supply chains, and ecological restoration with a One Health pedagogy. It navigated the challenges of a global pandemic and has influenced national building standards. These interwoven strategies demonstrate how a values-driven approach can produce resilient, scalable, and contextually grounded solutions. That's what makes it replicable—and powerful.

Anton Larsen Payá
Principal, MASS

Kelly Alvarez Doran
Co-Founder, Ha/f Climate Design,
(formerly) Principal, MASS

Sierra Bainbridge
Senior Principal & Managing Director, MASS

Chris Hardy
Design Director, MASS

Alan Ricks
Co-Executive Director & Founding Principal, MASS

Jean Paul Sebuhayi Uwase
Principal, MASS

MASS designed the RICA campus to heuristically demonstrate systems that could be understood and replicated by its students in form, function, and materiality long after they graduate. In this way, RICA's design is aligned with the broader campus pedagogy, prioritizing the One Health philosophy. The design prioritizes passive environmental strategies, such as natural ventilation and thermal mass and daylighting, to reduce energy consumption and negate the need for air-conditioning, and RICA is tracking to become the world's first climate-positive university, making a significant contribution to sustainable development and agriculture in Rwanda. The campus was built using local materials and sustainable methods, emphasizing environmental and social responsibility, workforce development, and economic growth.

H	Housing
D+G	Dairy Enterprise
P+S	Poultry and Swine Enterprise
C+E	Community and Extension
M+I	Mechanization and Irrigation Enterprise
R+F	Row and Forage Enterprise
V+T	Vegetable and Tree Crop Enterprise
FYF	First-Year Farms
WT	Wastewater Treatment Infiltration
SB	Swine Barns and Runs
LB	Small Livestock Barns
WC	Water Conservation Teaching Field
SW	Preserved Savannah Woodland
CP	Conservation Path
PF	Pivot Irrigation Demonstration Field
FO	Heritage Fruit Orchards
PW	Papyrus Wetland Edge
SF	Sports Field
PI	Large-Scale Pivot Irrigation
CC	Campus Center
SOL	Solar
REC	Recreation

Designing and Building the Rwanda Institute for Conservation Agriculture

Savannah Woodland

SOL
H
LB
WT
D+G
P+S
SB
WC
CP
C+E
SW
Mechanized
CC
V+T
R+F
PF
M+I
SF
REC
PI

Savannah Woodland

The intentional design of integrated ecological and agricultural systems within the campus promises to enhance productivity of crop output and the presence of biodiversity. This is achieved through four scales of ecosystem design that complement each other in function. These scales of ecosystem include agroforestry creating a layered agricultural planting system, marshland restoration along the lake edge, re-introduced native savannah woodland species, and the establishment of agricultural crops. While these interventions require maintenance for initial stabilization, once established their increased diversity begins to self-regulate, compounding benefits until an established ecosystem evolves. At this stage, maintenance transitions into stewardship and the impacts of a flourishing habitat can be seen through increased crop production, enhanced resilience to pests and disease, improved water and soil conditions, and human health and well-being.

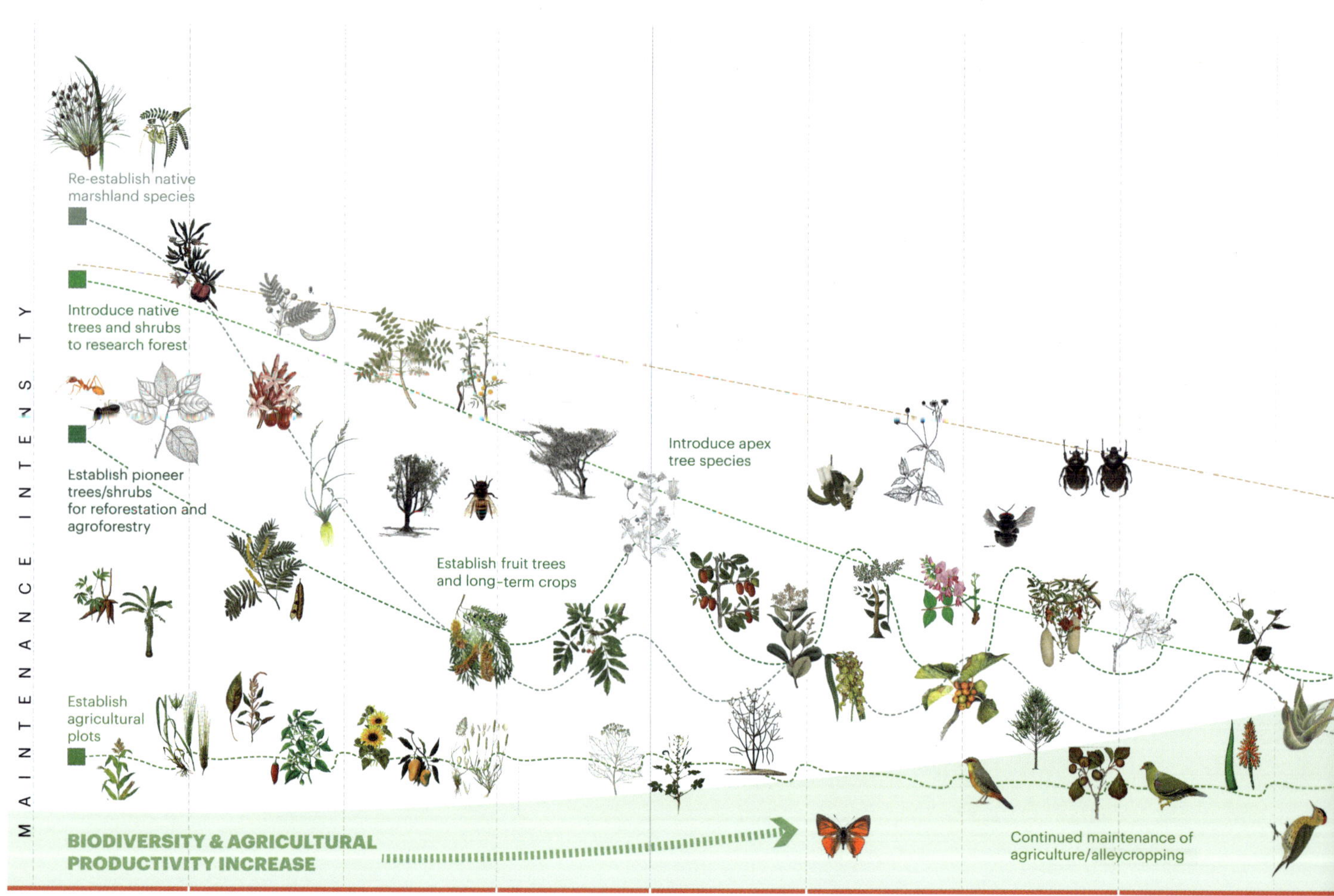

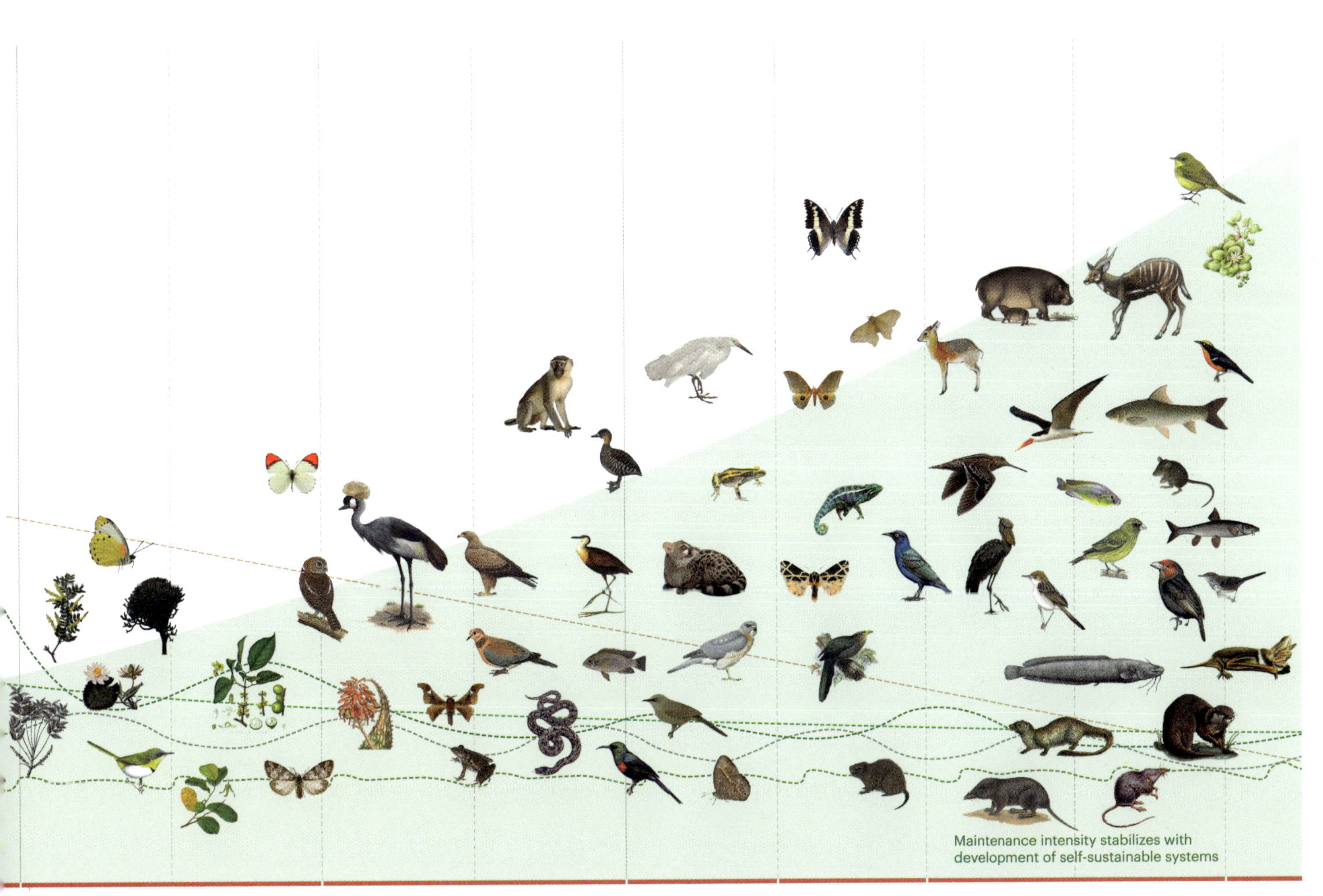
15+
Maintenance intensity stabilizes with
development of self-sustainable systems

Agriculture and ecology within the current landscapes of Rwanda are considered distinct from one another in land use, as they are in most of the world. Land is divided, categorized, and siloed—crops go here, livestock goes there—and this fragmentation disrupts the natural flows of people, water, animals, and knowledge. MASS believed that a different approach was possible at RICA to make curriculum and campus inseparable. The site was designed not simply to support learning, but to become the learning environment itself.

While most farmers in Rwanda today are smallholder farmers, the need for increased production will require enhanced output of diversified and processed crops. The design of the campus and curriculum embody this ambition, demonstrating how ecological and agricultural systems can be integrated for increased productivity and benefit. Over the course of three years, RICA's campus curriculum guides students from the fundamentals of running a small farm, to the cooperative scale, and into enhanced mechanization and processing. Each phase is spatially mapped into the campus—from the eastern housing zones for first-year farm life to the western enterprise and innovation clusters for co-op scale experimentation. The idea is that learning becomes a physical journey across the land, not reserved for the classroom.

MASS translated RICA's core, experiential learning mission into immersive agricultural and ecological systems. Moving along the central spine, students see a range of agricultural methodologies across the spectrum, from simple to complex. The impact of this approach seeks to train the next generation of farmers, expand cooperative members, spark entrepreneurial enterprises, and connect to the community. The goal is not only to grow food—but to grow a food system that is just, regenerative, and climate-resilient. In preparing students to live and lead within ecological limits, RICA's curriculum models the mindset of abundance: grounded, cooperative, and regenerative.

Learning Agriculture in a Progressive Curriculum

by **Therese Graf**

Planting design reinforces programming, operational clarity, and productive flows at RICA. Each strip of land is a living experiment in how diversity builds resilience, how care regenerates soil, and how balance returns when native species are given space to thrive. Each planting approach reflects the functions of the space as well as the diversity of species that support it. The stormwater slices provide clear ecological connectivity through the site while providing habitat. The housing and social spaces offer restored canopy cover and gardens with aesthetic value. The fields create functional spaces of cultivation and production, reflecting a diverse and symbiotic relationship between the range of uses and the species that are dependent upon them.

This enlarged plan of the strips near the second- and third-year housing building and the first-year farm offers a demonstration of the planting approach. The first strip demonstrates a unique condition of stormwater treatment basins capturing the water from uphill and slowing it for enhanced infiltration. The second strip offers an event lawn for recreational use, educational sessions, and gathering by the students directly off the spine path. The central strips provide ecological value as native grass collections, which highlight species of interest for both habitat and aesthetic value. Finally, a basketball court is integrated within silviculture planting in the last strip, blending agricultural production of timber with spaces for students from the adjacent houses to come and play. Each of these strips integrates a unique selection of species tied to their intended performance, while also creating a dynamic condition along the spine for experiential learning.

MASS embraced the diversity of species that are native to the woodland savannah ecotype of the region to create a landscape for this site, exploring their connections and considering how they support one another in proliferation through time. The campus's central strips are the heart of the design, serving as a series of plots dedicated to native ecosystem regeneration, recreation, and agricultural testing. Each strip has a unique design approach that highlights a variety of experiential and educational programming opportunities that tie directly to how landscape composition and management can be optimized for a range of benefits and can become complementary. They also provide space for testing and adaptation over time, at a scale that is more flexible and manageable in comparison to the larger agricultural fields and production areas.

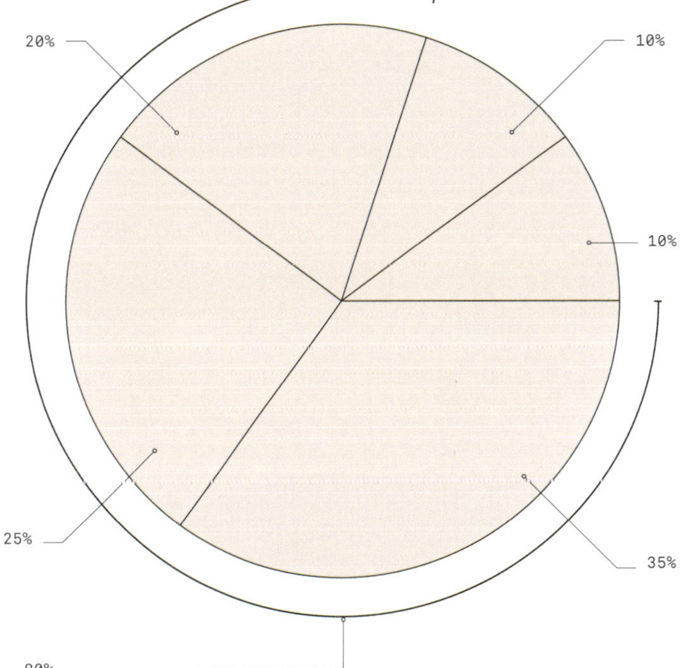

Rwanda Institute for
Conservation Agriculture
Designing Curriculum

YR 1 Smallholder Farm

In Year 1, students
live together with 20
classmates on a 5 acre (2.1
hectare) plot, immersed
in a smallholder farmer's
experience, learning to
diversify and intensify
agriculture.

YR 2 & 3 Enterprises Scale

In Year 2, students confront
the challenge of five
"enterprises," learning
value-add agriculture, and
moving raw harvest to final
process and sale. In Year 3,
students develop specialized
expertise in two enterprises
and work with communities on
a practicum project.

The enterprises are:
• Vegetable & tree crops
• Mechanization & irrigation
• Row & forage crops
• Dairy
• Poultry & swine

Impact

80% of graduates become
entrepreneurs, impacting
future agricultural
development on local
and national scales.

35%   Farm operators

25%   Manage co-ops

20%   Commercial enterprises
       supporting farmers

10%   Gov/policy

10%   Grad school/educators

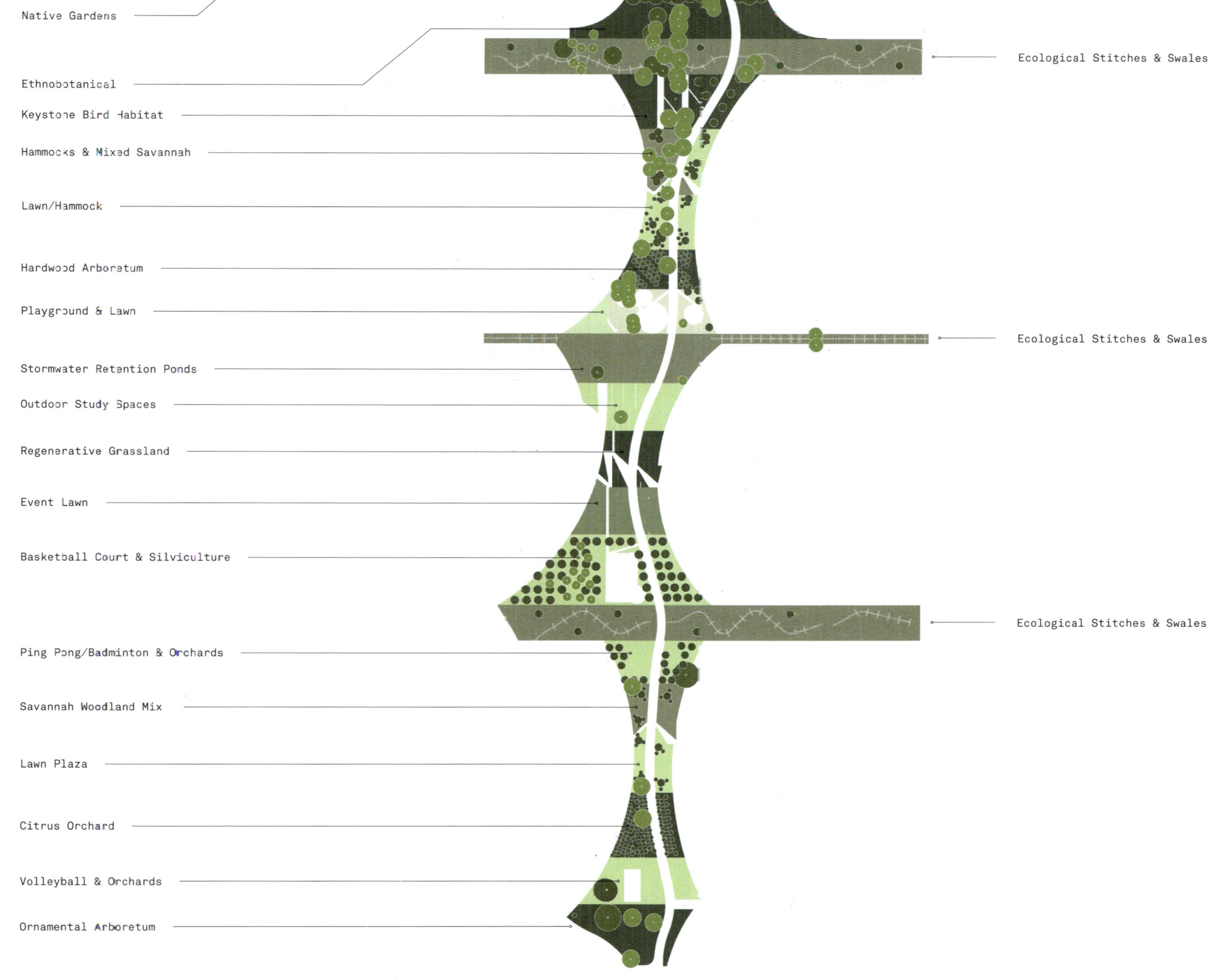

Native Gardens
Ethnobotanical
Keystone Bird Habitat
Hammocks & Mixed Savannah
Lawn/Hammock
Hardwood Arboretum
Playground & Lawn
Stormwater Retention Ponds
Outdoor Study Spaces
Regenerative Grassland
Event Lawn
Basketball Court & Silviculture
Ping Pong/Badminton & Orchards
Savannah Woodland Mix
Lawn Plaza
Citrus Orchard
Volleyball & Orchards
Ornamental Arboretum
Ecological Stitches & Swales
Ecological Stitches & Swales
Ecological Stitches & Swales

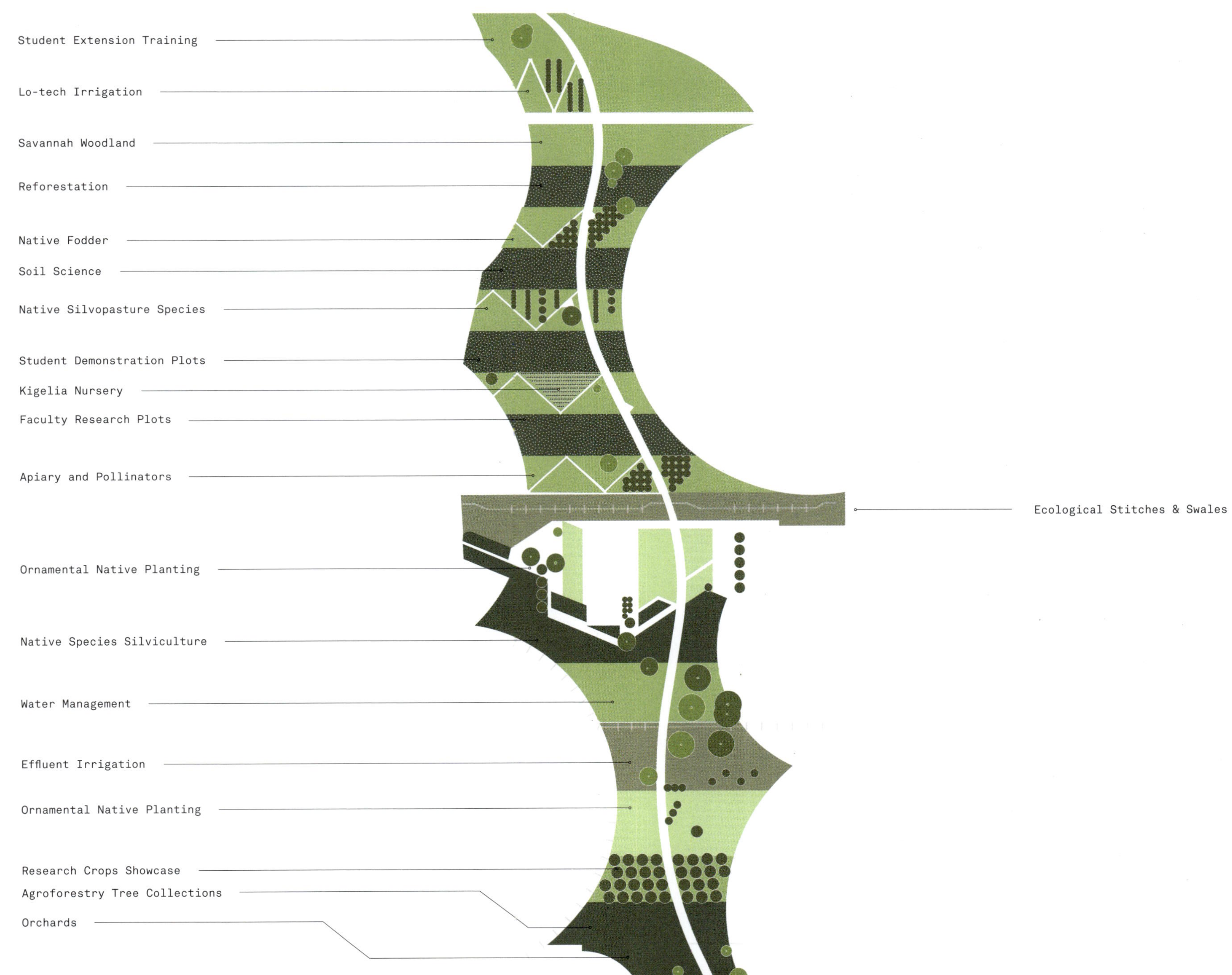

Student Extension Training
Lo-tech Irrigation
Savannah Woodland
Reforestation
Native Fodder
Soil Science
Native Silvopasture Species
Student Demonstration Plots
Kigelia Nursery
Faculty Research Plots
Apiary and Pollinators
Ecological Stitches & Swales
Ornamental Native Planting
Native Species Silviculture
Water Management
Effluent Irrigation
Ornamental Native Planting
Research Crops Showcase
Agroforestry Tree Collections
Orchards

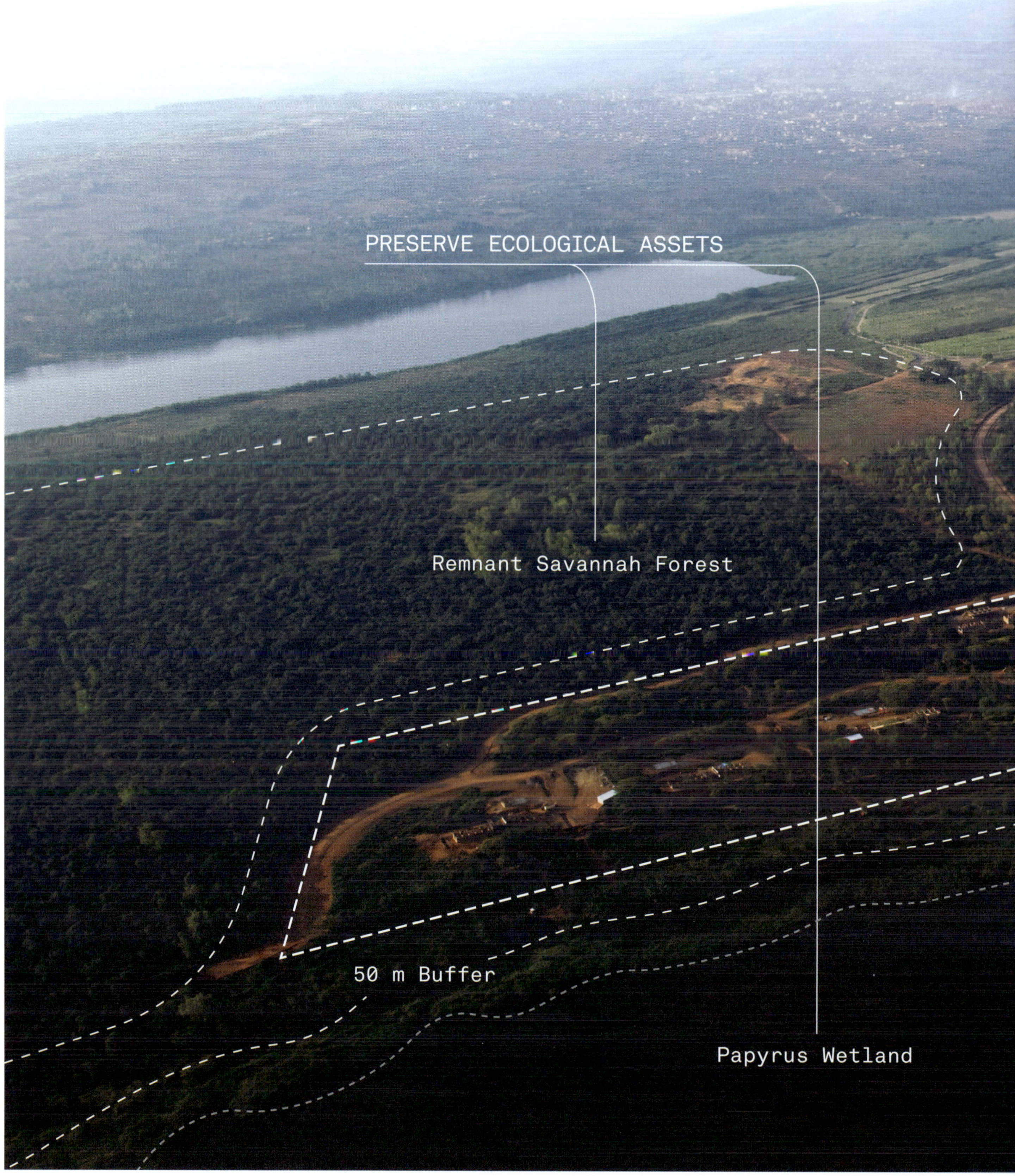
PRESERVE ECOLOGICAL ASSETS
Remnant Savannah Forest
50 m Buffer
Papyrus Wetland

SITING BASED ON SOIL & SLOPE
Best Grazing
Remnant Savannah Forest
Best Soils

Savannah Woodland

Papyrus Ecosystem
- Establish buffer zone for construction
- Restore grey crowned crane (and other apex species habitat)
- Retain existing trees to stabilize soils
- Preserve papyrus

First-Year Farms
- Replicate smallholder experience
- Preserve existing orchard varietals
- Support small livestock and agroforestry techniques
- Build soil health

Recreation & Social Areas
- Locate passive and active social spaces aligned with existing tree groves
- Provide sport courts
- Provide study spaces and hammock groves

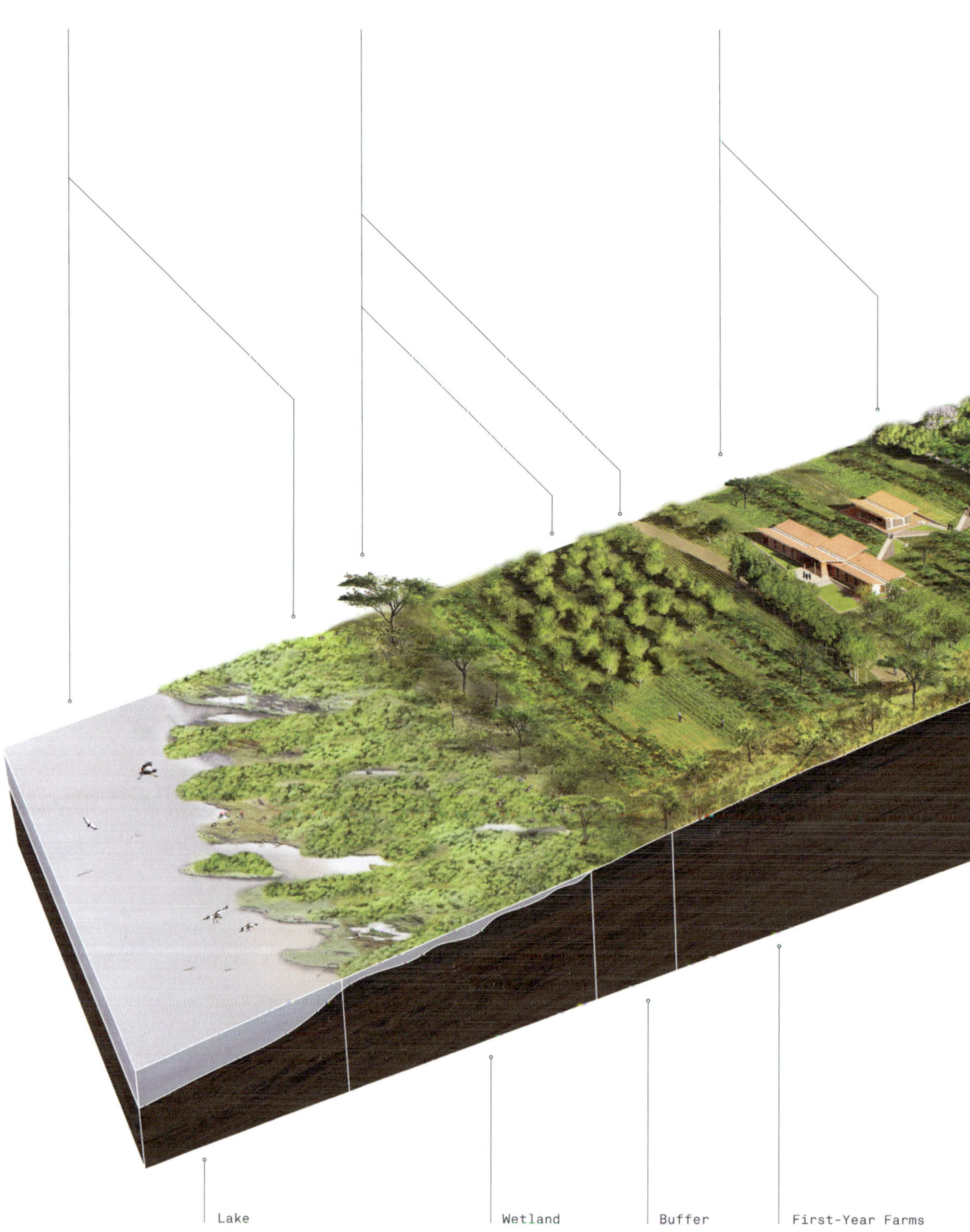

Savannah Woodland

Water Management
- Slow stormwater through planted swales
- Allow for future rooftop water collection
- Reduce erosion and siltation
- Increase infiltration

Ecology Stitch
- Connect lake and papyrus with savannah
- Provide pollinator gardens and native habitats
- Establish wind barriers

Conservation Areas
- Preserve existing biophilia
- Increase density of native plantings

Spine

Faculty Housing

Conservation Preserve

RICA's first-year students live and work on a smallholder farm to understand and experience this model of agriculture, which accounts for 80 percent of Rwanda's farms. Each first-year farm consists of a two-acre plot and hosts up to twenty-one students, building cohorts and community. Housing for second- and third-year students also fosters impromptu exchanges and collaboration, helping them forge the networks that will serve them well after graduation, leading successful cooperatives in the Bugesera District and throughout Rwanda.

By integrating regenerative architecture with hands-on education, the campus fosters solutions to climate change and food insecurity, while strengthening local communities.

Savannah Woodland

The zoning of agricultural production aims for optimal use by each class of about eighty to ninety students, integrating buildings and landscapes—not only as a matter of efficiency but as a matter of pedagogy. For example, a large irrigation pivot is located between the row and forage and the mechanization and irrigation enterprises, allowing students to interface directly with the fields from the classrooms and laboratories.

This approach leverages site and environmental conditions by reconnecting ecological assets and creating corridors with demonstration plots and activity spaces. Earthen walls symbolize the importance of soil health in agriculture. Timber used for roof construction is a product of silviculture, harvested and processed for sale. Clay tile roofs shelter the structure below and are kiln fired using agricultural waste—coffee husks left over from Rwanda's main export. These all represent the transformation of raw materials into something more refined and, ultimately, more valuable—as crop harvests become sustenance for a growing population. The Bugesera District is also a prime location for solar energy gain in Rwanda, so RICA is completely powered by an on-site 1.5 MW solar array and battery storage.

Our first design principle was preservation—celebrating the existing ecological assets that are the backbone of RICA, as both an institution and a regional example of regenerative design. Soil quality and slope conditions shaped the agricultural programs and the design of the campus, whose plan includes landscapes, housing, classrooms, meeting rooms, barn storage, waste management systems for both humans and animals, and off-grid energy infrastructure. Students live and work enmeshed in the campus laboratory, and carry forward the One Health curriculum into the agricultural enterprises they will hopefully begin after graduation.

The large site and conservation agricultural activities provide the grounds for achieving a climate- and nature-positive project. Our team of architects and engineers worked to reduce the upfront embodied carbon impacts of the project to 40 percent of a business-as-usual case by harvesting much of the project's materials from the site itself and by reducing the use of carbon-intensive materials like cement and steel as much as possible. We worked with nature, rather than against it, to minimize active systems for water and energy, reducing the size of the solar farm and water treatment facilities that support the off-grid campus. The buildings are cooled and breathe passively. Water is managed on-site through swales, and trees provide shade and shelter. This results in a dramatically reduced carbon and nature footprint—which can be turned into a positive one within twenty years through on-site afforestation, silviculture, and conservation agriculture practices—resulting in Africa's first climate-positive campus.

Savannah Woodland

First-, second-, and third-year students live the ideals they are learning by enjoying locally grown and prepared food. The structure of the cafeteria and the rest of the campus is composed largely of biogenic materials, including rammed earth, compressed earth blocks, wood, stone, and terra-cotta, which are durable, replicable, and repairable.

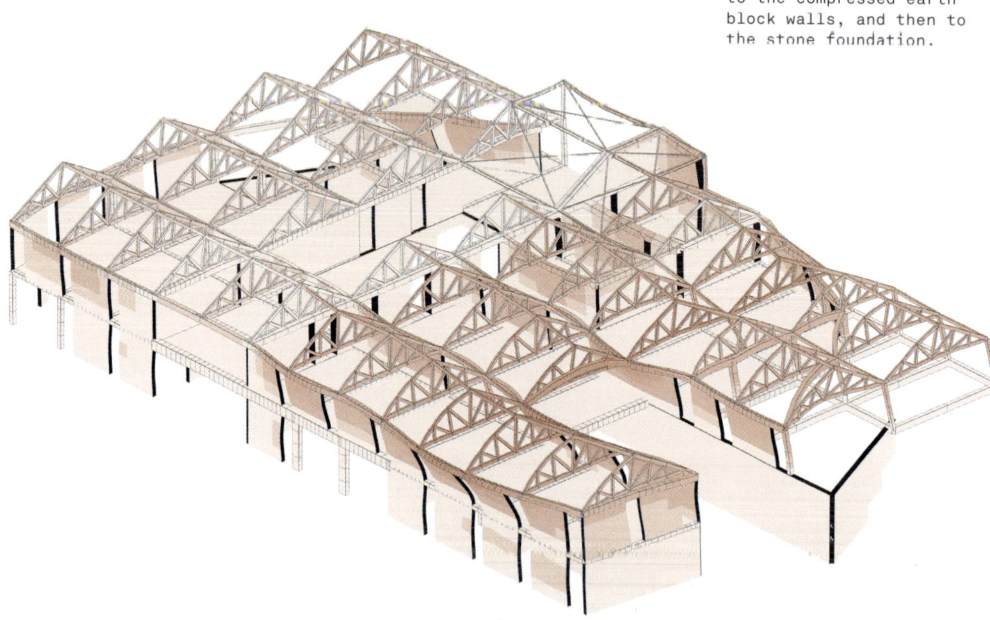

This diagram reveals how MASS expected the building to move during a seismic event, which are common in this region. The lateral forces of the roof transfer to the compressed earth block walls, and then to the stone foundation.

Savannah Woodland

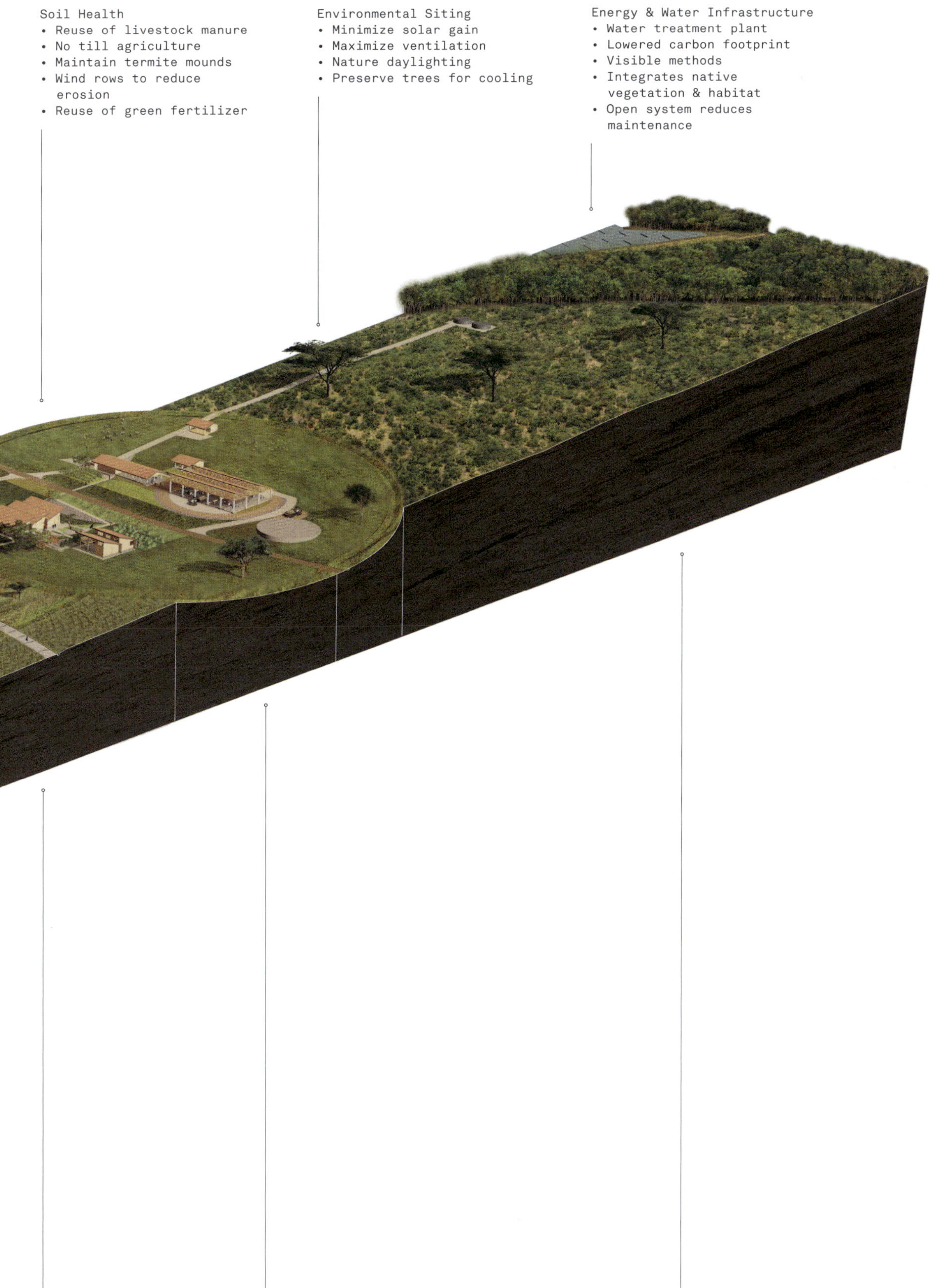

Soil Health
• Reuse of livestock manure
• No till agriculture
• Maintain termite mounds
• Wind rows to reduce erosion
• Reuse of green fertilizer

Environmental Siting
• Minimize solar gain
• Maximize ventilation
• Nature daylighting
• Preserve trees for cooling

Energy & Water Infrastructure
• Water treatment plant
• Lowered carbon footprint
• Visible methods
• Integrates native vegetation & habitat
• Open system reduces maintenance

Spine
Enterprise: Dairy
Pasture

Analysis Layer
Element list: all not PS
Scale: 1:66.30
Highlighted:
Coincident Nodes
Coincident Elements
Deformation magnification
Elem. Trans., Uz: 100.00 n
Output axis: local

    21.10 mm
    16.96 mm
    12.82 mm
     8.69 mm
     4.55 mm
     0.42 mm
  - 3.72 mm
     7.86 mm
  - 11.99 mm
  - 16.12 mm
  - 20.26 mm
  - 24.40 mm
  - 28.53 mm
  - 32.67 mm
  - 36.80 mm
  - 40.94 mm
  - 45.07 mm
  - 49.21 mm
  - 53.35 mm
  - 57.48 mm

Case: A3 : d + l

The wooden trusses used at RICA were simple to build and easy to replicate, and were designed to span 8 m. Their 4 m heights utilize regionally sourced timbers, allowing MASS to achieve larger climate goals for the project.

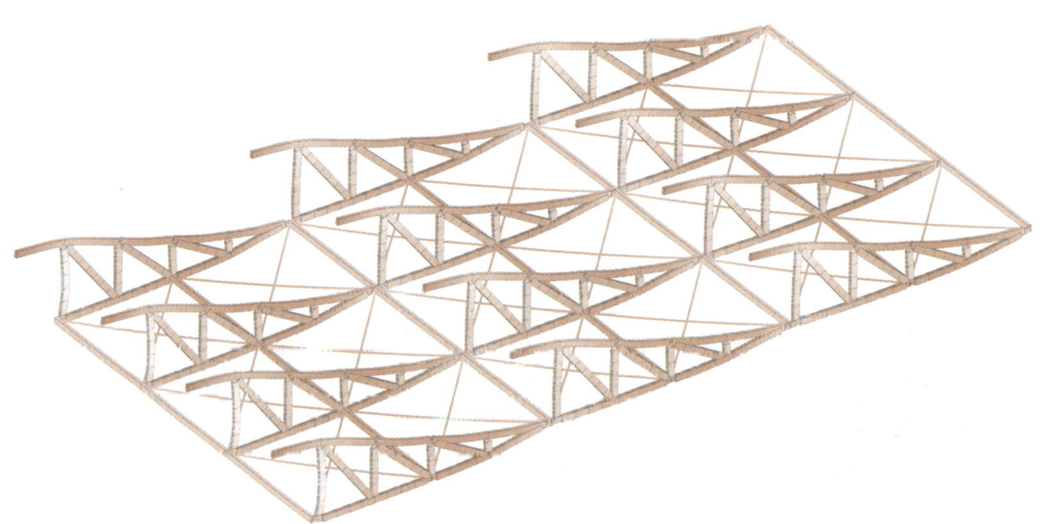

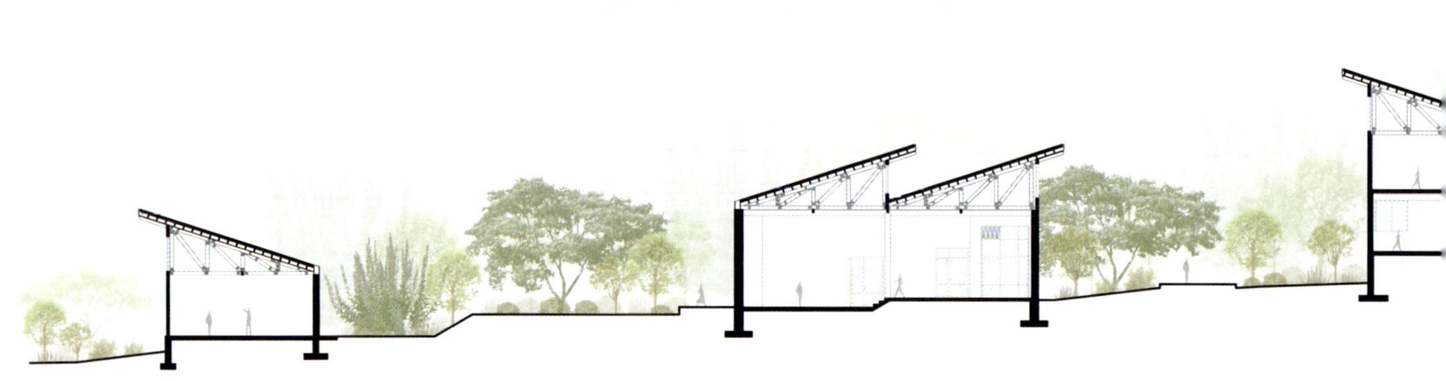

Savannah Woodland

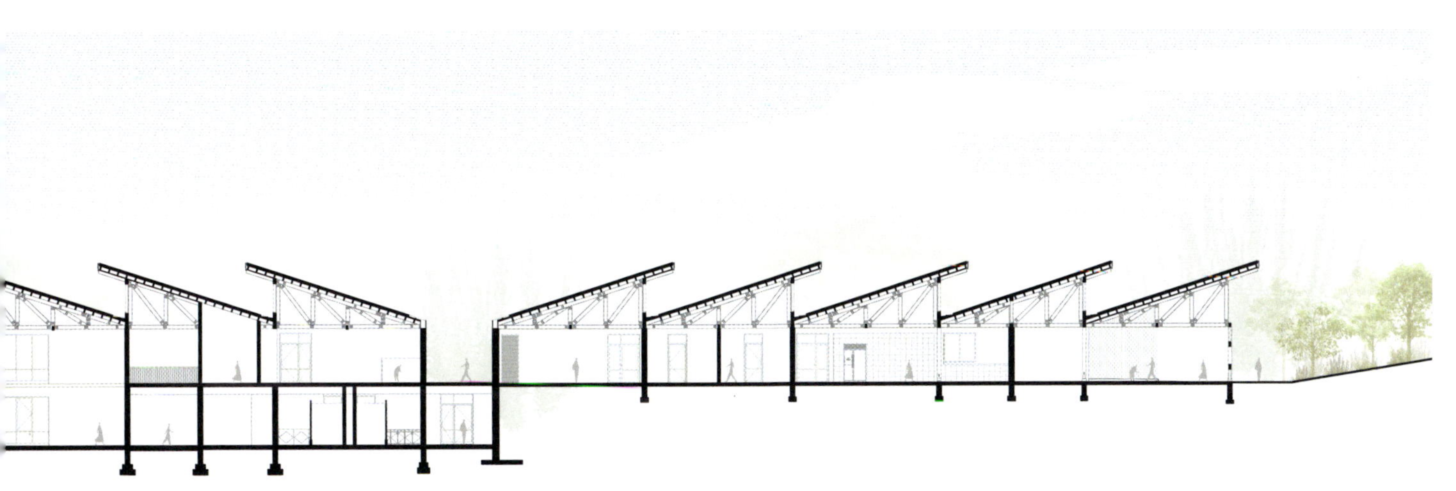

By using regionally
sourced and elemental
materials like earth,
stone, and wood, MASS
drove down the embodied
carbon footprint of
RICA to less than half
of a project that uses
conventional construction
in East Africa.

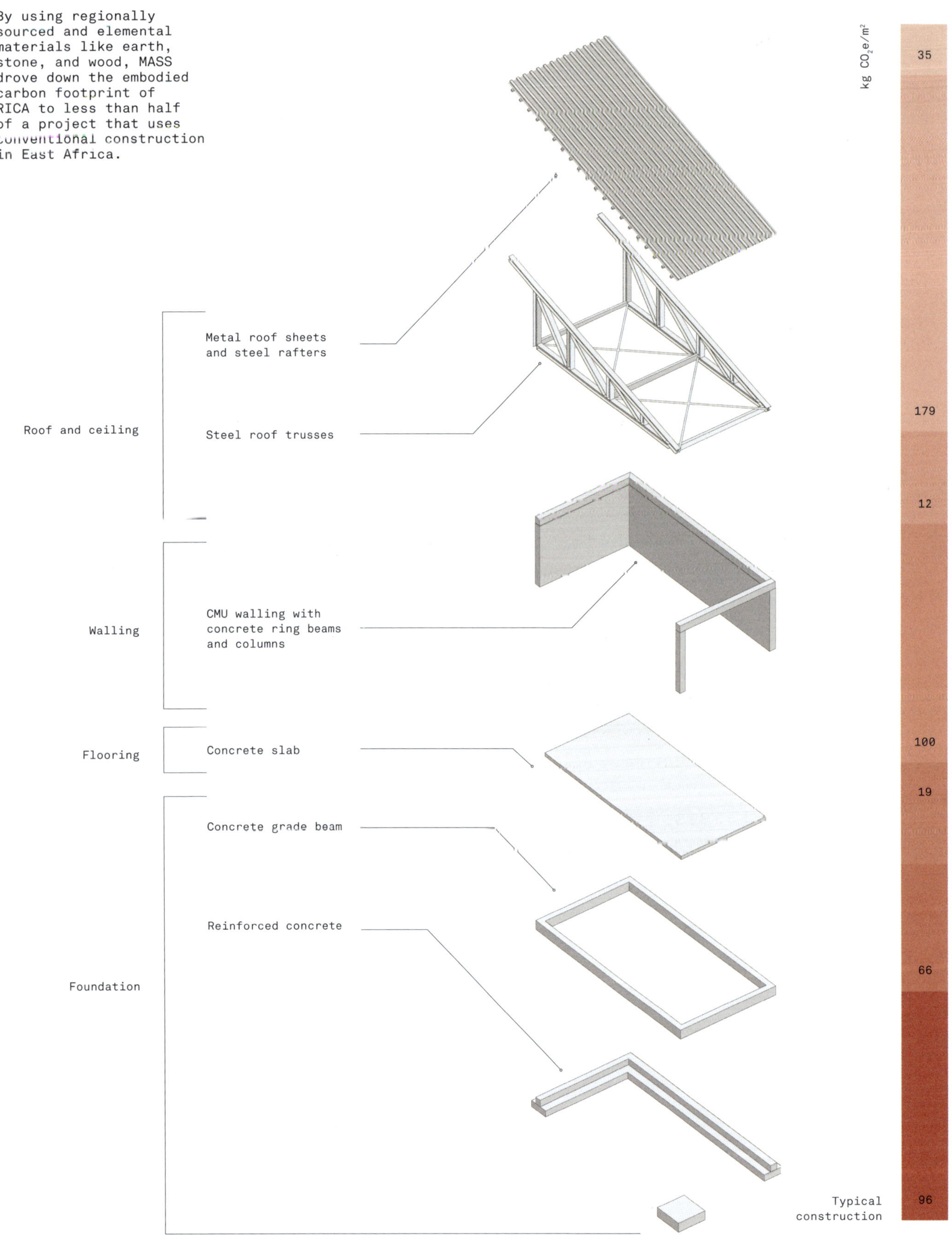

Savannah Woodland

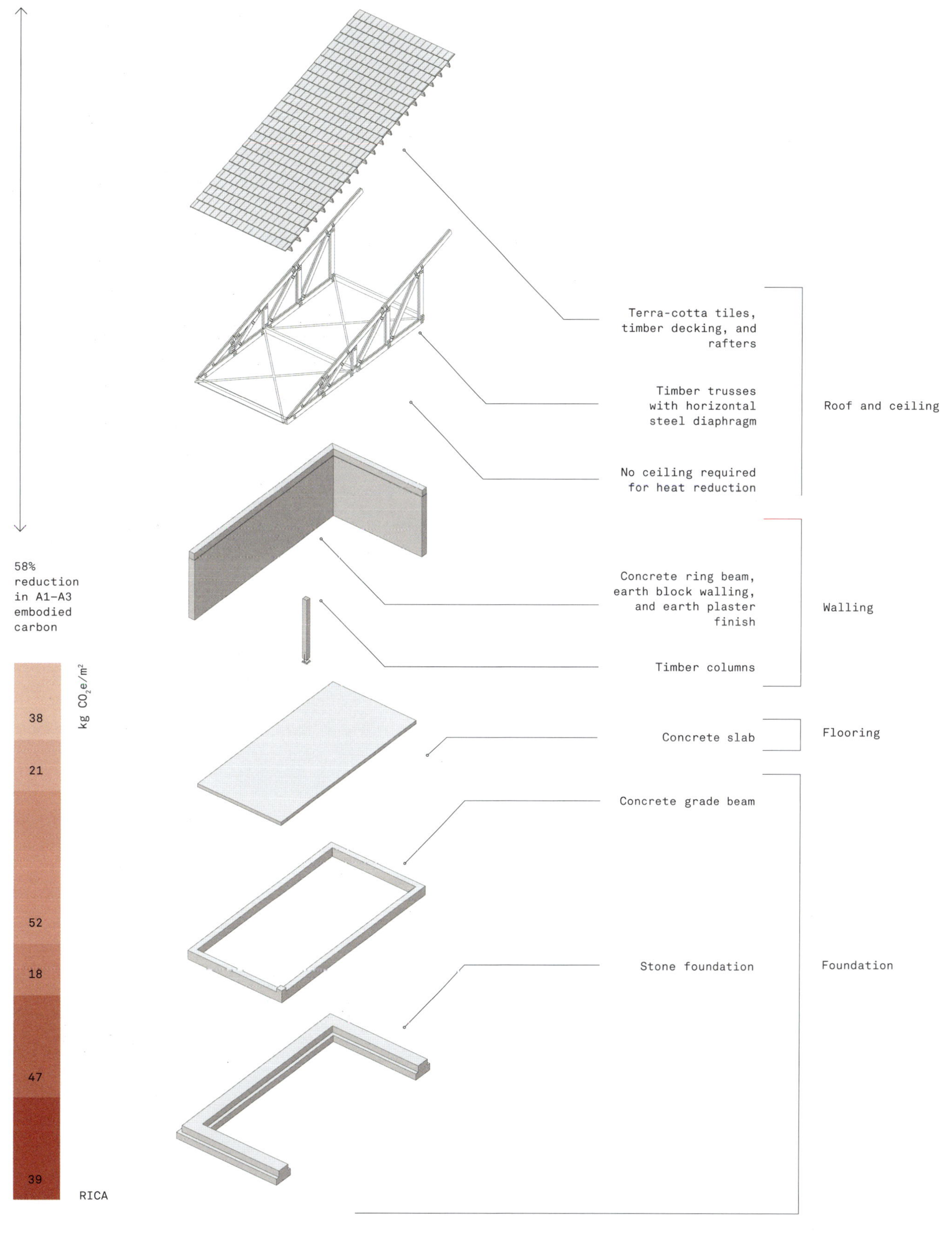

58% reduction in A1–A3 embodied carbon

kg CO$_2$e/m^2

38
21
52
18
47
39

RICA

Terra-cotta tiles, timber decking, and rafters

Timber trusses with horizontal steel diaphragm

No ceiling required for heat reduction

Roof and ceiling

Concrete ring beam, earth block walling, and earth plaster finish

Timber columns

Walling

Concrete slab

Flooring

Concrete grade beam

Stone foundation

Foundation

Savannah Woodland

Case Studies

Protecting a Renewable Resource

Foundations for the Future

How to Repurpose Soil for Walls

Earth Elevated to Craft

Forging a Purpose-Built and Handmade Future

Plant sourcing for the project was an extensive effort, requiring us to procure and propagate over one million plants. The species list integrated native species that had ecological value as well as agricultural value. Some of these species were common or well known within the region, but a number required thorough planning and investigation. An on-site nursery was used for plant propagation, while other plants were sourced directly from the adjacent fields and farmers. Sites where the expansive cover offered a source for splitting and direct transplanting plants without negative impact to the existing ecology were leveraged as much as possible, especially with grass species.

A central aspect of RICA's design is its integration with the local community and economy. MASS's construction process actively involved local workers, training over three hundred artisans in crafts ranging from weaving to rammed earth. Within a workforce of 1,200 people, nine out of ten came from the Bugesera district, where the project site is located. Overall, 90 percent of the project budget was spent within five hundred miles. This focus on local labor and resources not only supports the regional economy but also fosters knowledge transfer, ensures the campus is readily maintainable, and overall reflects the values of the place in how it is built. The campus layout reflects RICA's dual mission of education and environmental conservation. Academic buildings are strategically placed to optimize views, airflow, and access to the agricultural fields, where students engage in hands-on learning, as seen in the following spread.

Savannah Woodland

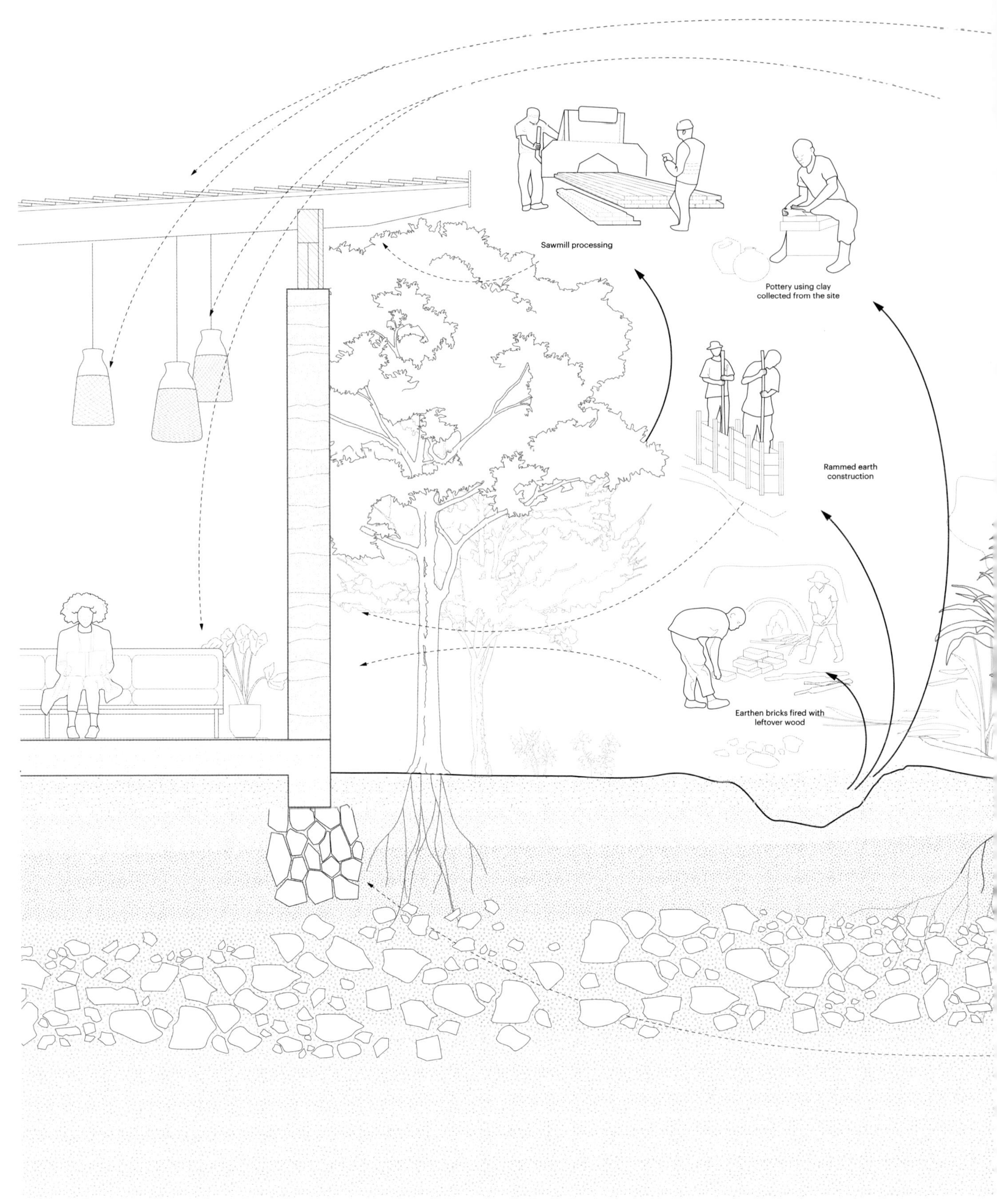

Sawmill processing
Pottery using clay collected from the site
Rammed earth construction
Earthen bricks fired with leftover wood

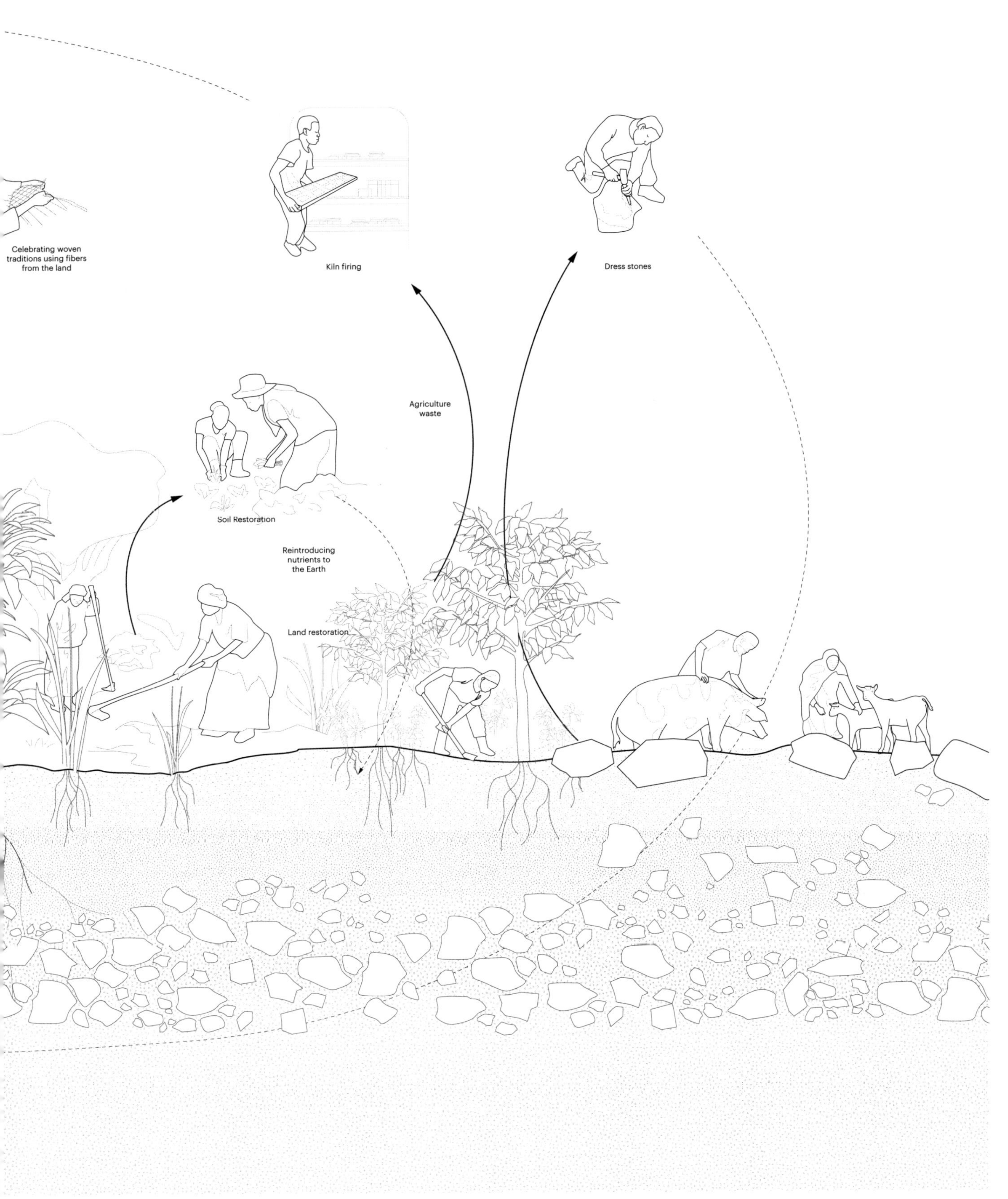

Celebrating woven
traditions using fibers
from the land
Kiln firing
Dress stones
Soil Restoration
Agriculture
waste
Reintroducing
nutrients to
the Earth
Land restoration

While Rwanda has a long history of forestry and rotational timber harvest managed by the department of forestry, this wood had never been sawn, kiln-dried, or graded for nominal, rectilinear structural lumber. Using wood as a primary part of the structure may seem like a counterintuitive decision when confronting widespread deforestation in Rwanda. However, we felt that being able to demonstrate the possibility of sustainable forestry and construction would be a catalyst for further investment in both reforestation and industry in the country. Silviculture, for example could become a significant new program helping to improve biodiversity, while also becoming a more sustainable construction industry supply chain when compared to carbon-intensive imported products like cement and steel.

Through extensive research we identified native species that through reforestation could contribute to restoring the health of deforested areas, as well as function as ideal structural materials for buildings and furniture. Thoughtful deployment of this strategy represents a stronger One Health approach, especially as compared to prior reforestation efforts that used eucalyptus. While fast growing—the reason it was initially used—eucalyptus is an exotic species that depletes soil of nutrients and water and serves little ecological benefit since other species don't recognize it as habitat.

A range of timber species were assessed for structural, architectural, and furniture applications across the project, with a primary focus on native species, while also considering those available in large quantities through sustainable forestry. Although not native to the region, *Pinus patula* was selected to be used as structural timber for the project due to it being widely cultivated within sustainably managed forests across sub-Saharan Africa, including within an existing buffer zone around Nyungwe Forest National Park in the southwest region of Rwanda.

MASS selected native hardwood species including *Markhamia lutea* (umusave) for furniture and finish carpentry. These species are fast growing and harvested by hand on a community level, minimizing impact on the forest. They also represent species that are ecologically beneficial and could be key parts of future reforestation programs. Working with wood asks us to think generationally: not just about what we cut but what we grow. In this way, timber becomes a living measure of abundance—when forest health, craft, and climate resilience align.

MASS pursued modularity in the layout of the buildings to enhance efficiency and minimize waste. The standard eight-by-four-meter grid was selected based on the maximum length of timbers that can fit in drying kilns. This limited offcut waste and simplified fabrication—both reducing cost. MASS designed truss connections for ease of assembly, using bolted joints with steel plates, which could double as a template for bolt hole positioning during the fabrication process and ensuring consistency and replicability across multiple buildings. Assessing the strength of the timber for structural use was a complex and extensive process. Given the limited data available, we decided to strength-test a set of samples from every batch delivered to site.

The timber was first sorted into two custom visual grades based primarily on the quantity and arrangement of knots found across the cross section. These samples were then tested to destruction in a materials laboratory using an adapted concrete crushing machine, recording both loads applied and the deflection. Over five hundred individual specimens were tested from five sawmills across the region. The results were statistically analyzed to establish the fifth-percentile strength and stiffness properties that are required for structural design in accordance with Eurocodes. Testing revealed significant variability in timber quality even within the same visual grade and from the same sawmills, emphasizing the importance of rigorous selection and classification.

**Protecting
a Renewable
Resource**

**by
Cam Bailey**

Through this process, we have been able to demonstrate that regionally sourced timber, when carefully graded and tested, can serve as a reliable structural material in East Africa. However, the supply chain would greatly benefit from a few key interventions, such as longer-term forest management—not to mention agricultural education—strength-testing at the source to avoid processing of noncompliant timber, and utilizing natural treatment methods.

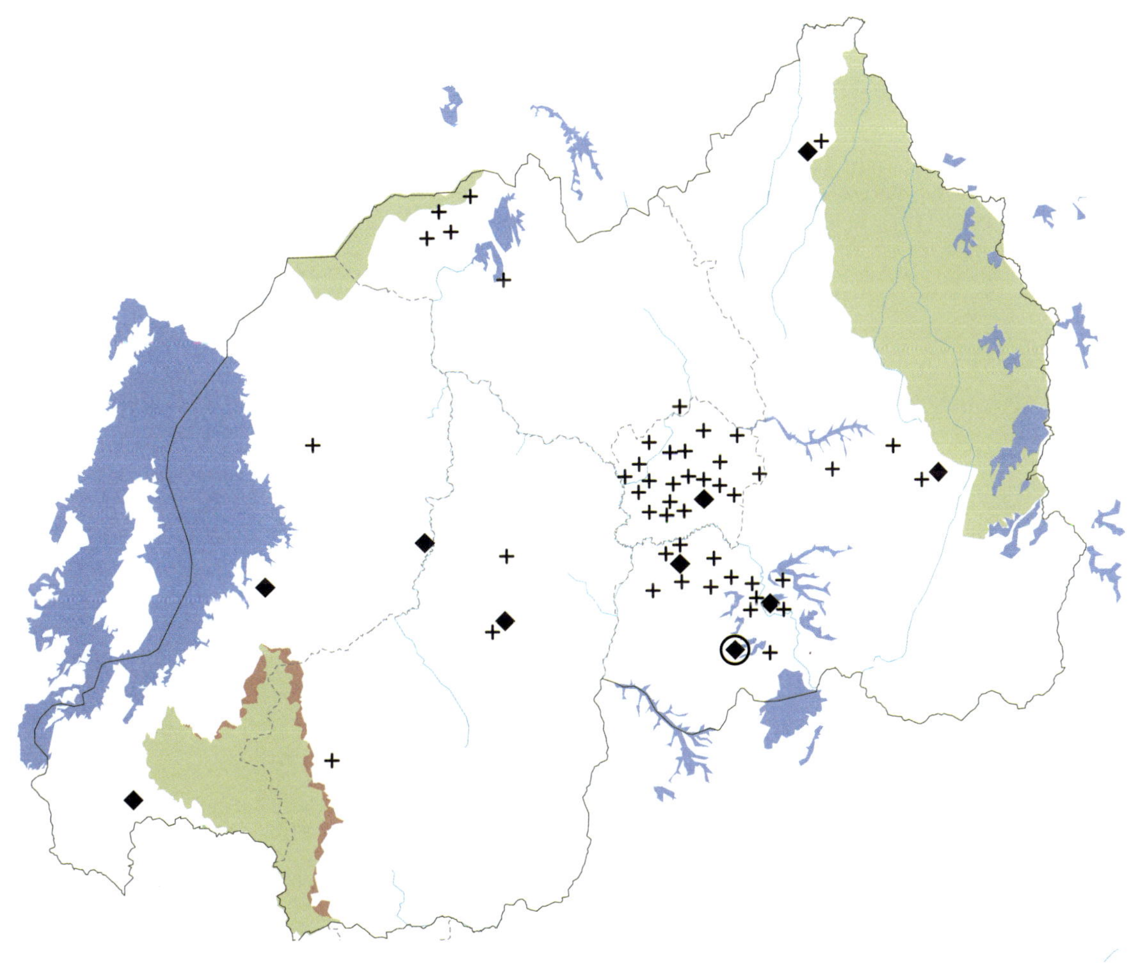

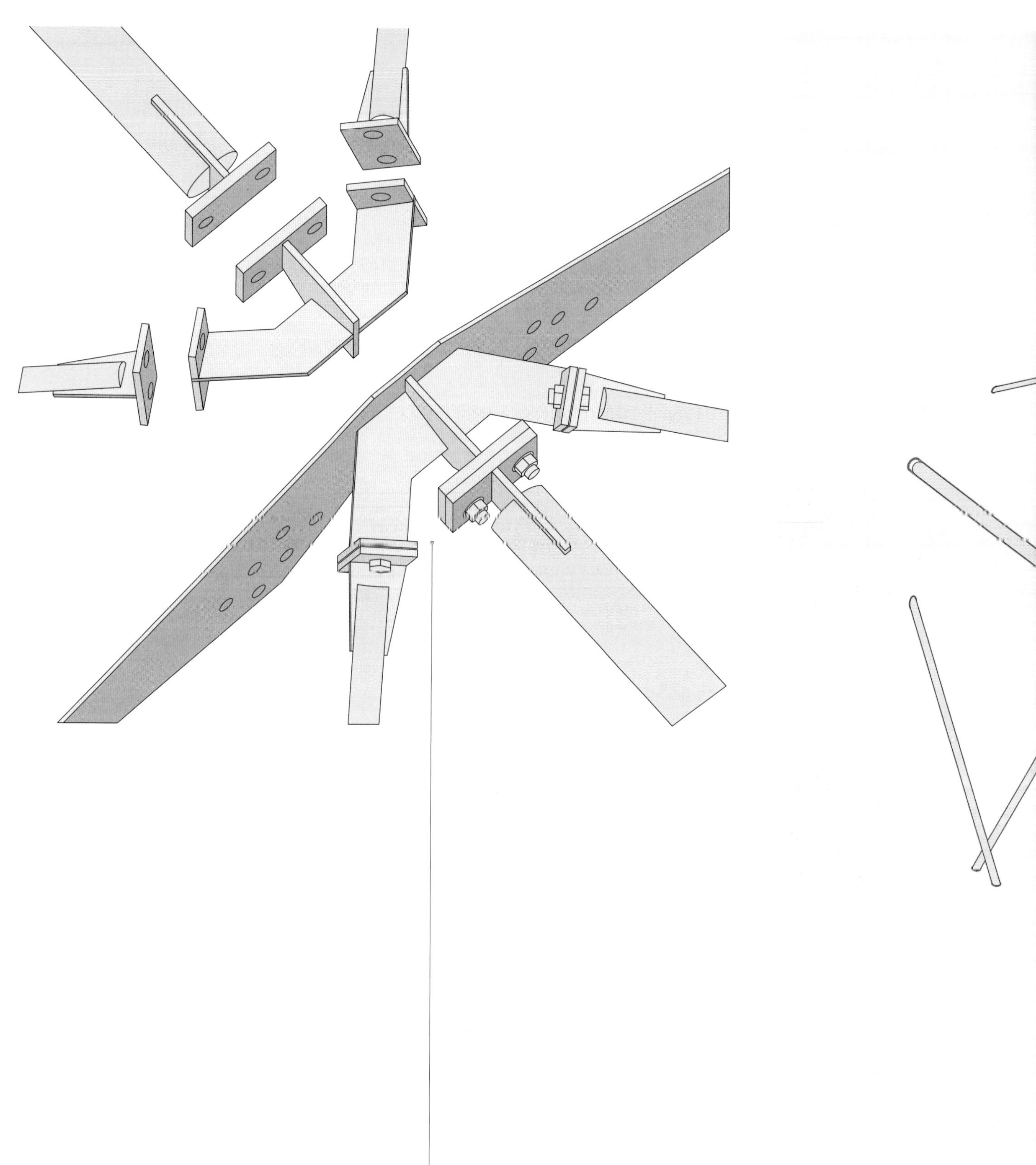

Complex steel connections
were fabricated in Kigali
and Nairobi.

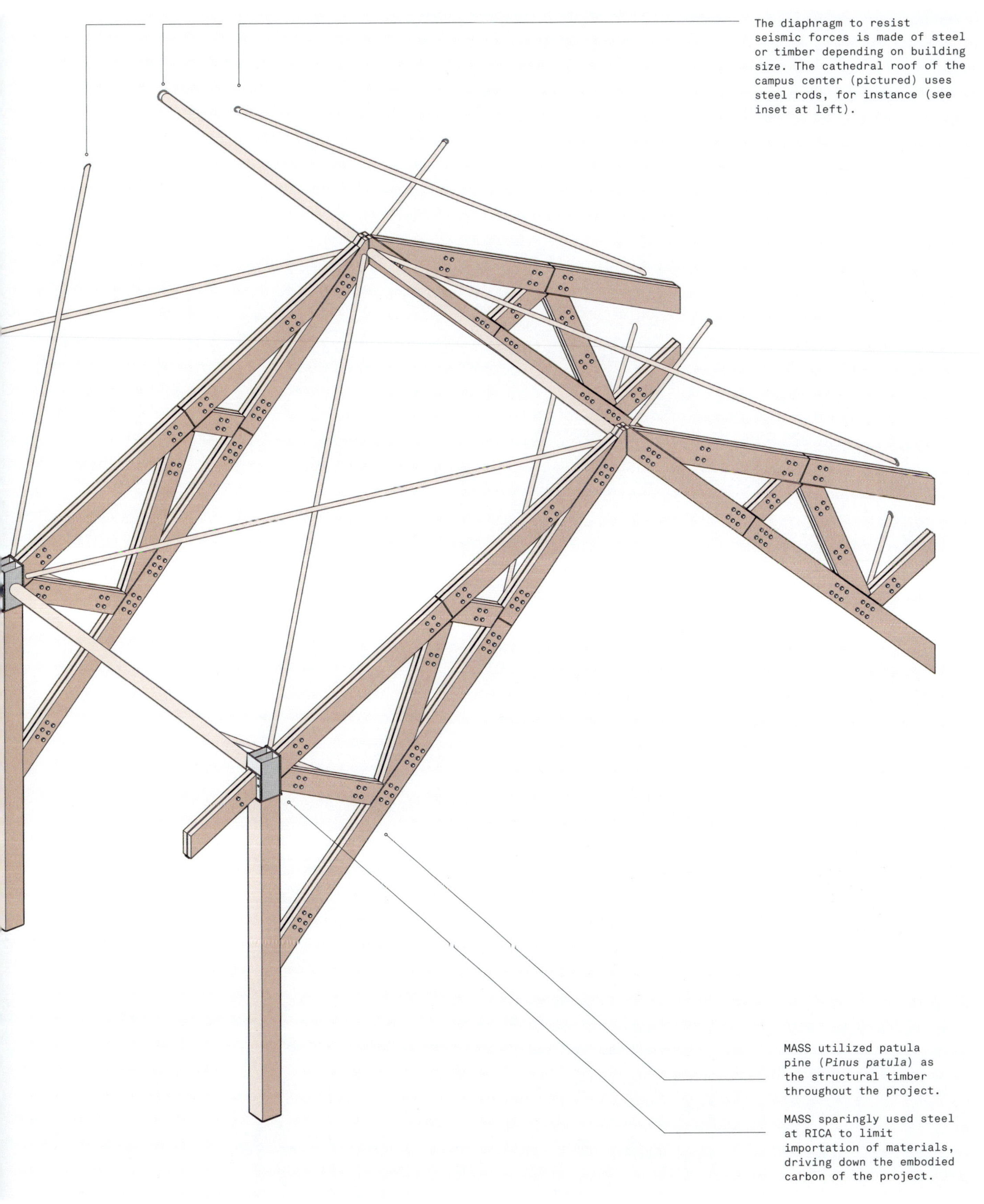

The diaphragm to resist seismic forces is made of steel or timber depending on building size. The cathedral roof of the campus center (pictured) uses steel rods, for instance (see inset at left).

MASS utilized patula pine (*Pinus patula*) as the structural timber throughout the project.

MASS sparingly used steel at RICA to limit importation of materials, driving down the embodied carbon of the project.

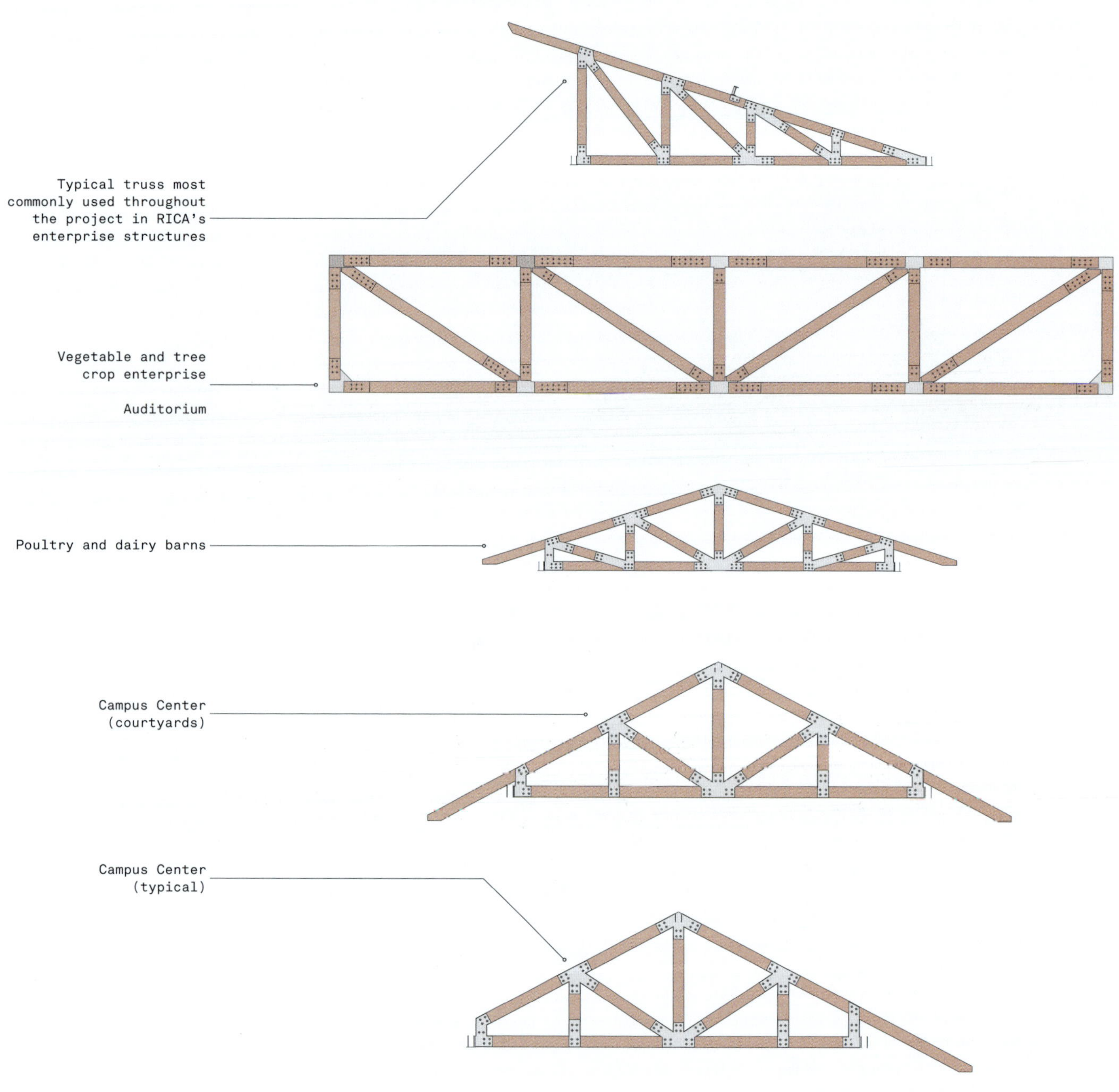
Typical truss most commonly used throughout the project in RICA's enterprise structures
Vegetable and tree crop enterprise
Auditorium
Poultry and dairy barns
Campus Center (courtyards)
Campus Center (typical)

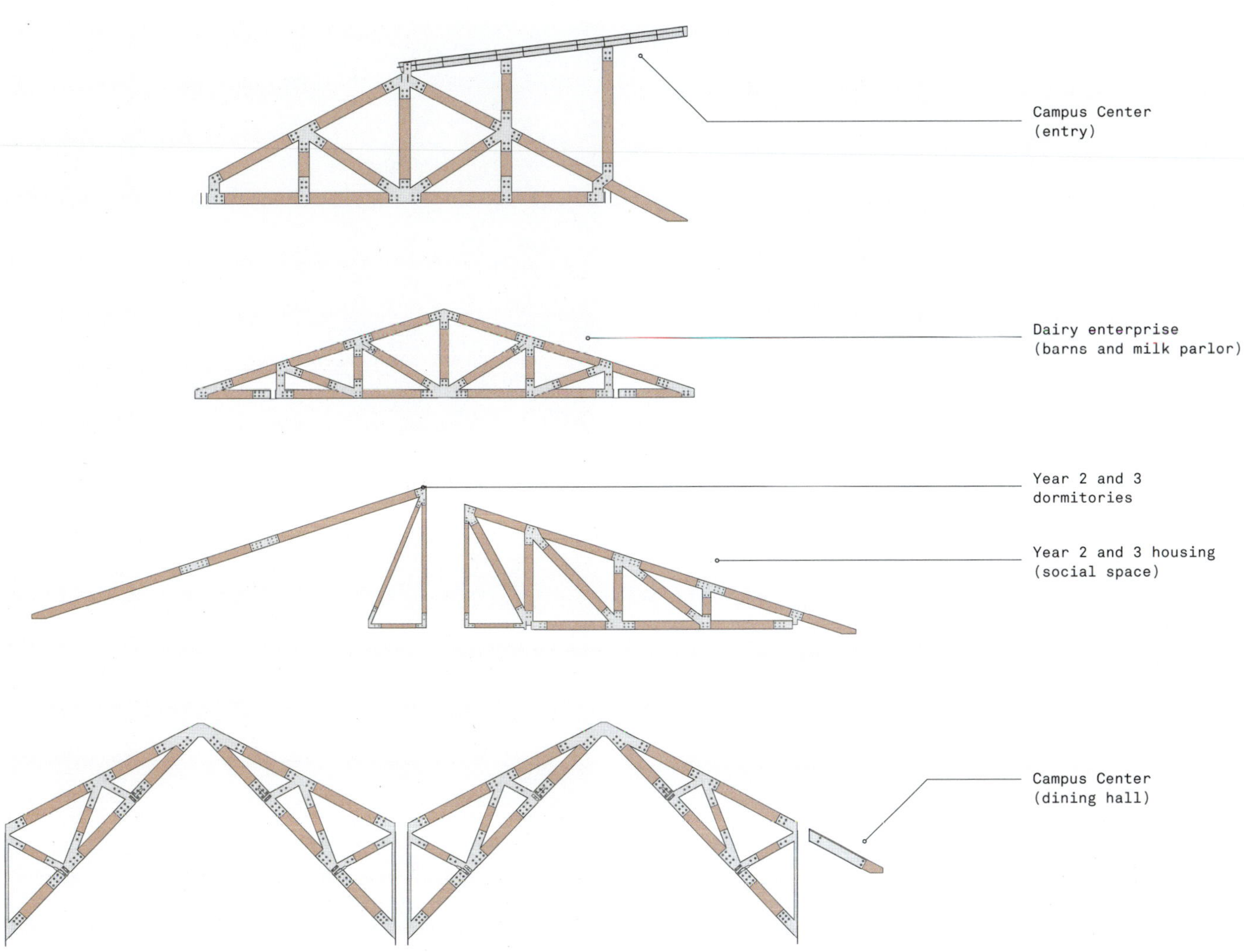

Campus Center
(entry)

Dairy enterprise
(barns and milk parlor)

Year 2 and 3
dormitories

Year 2 and 3 housing
(social space)

Campus Center
(dining hall)

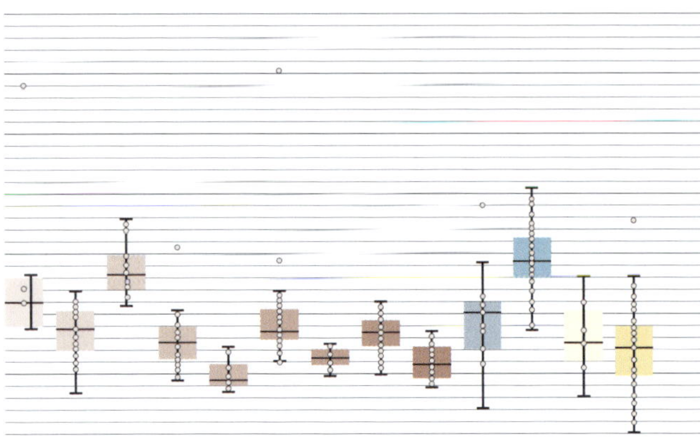

Box and Whisker Plots for Modulus of Elasticity
(including outliers)

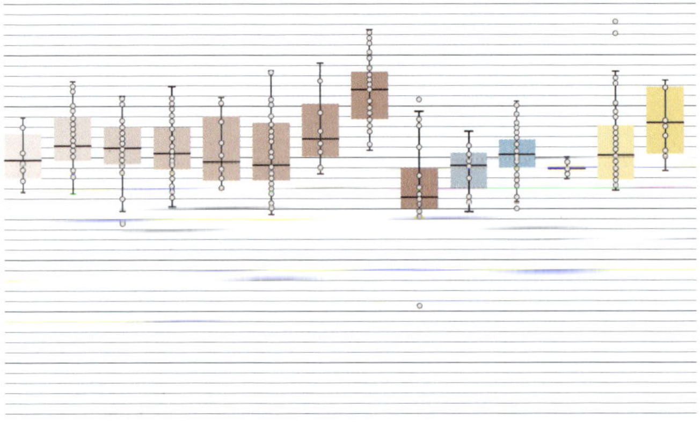

Box and Whisker Plots for Density
(including outliers)

MASS tested hundreds of samples from regional suppliers and
graded each sample based on its best use, dramatically reducing
waste in the project. Grade 1 (brown) were ideal for long spans,
Grade 2 (blue) for joists and columns, and ungraded (yellow)
were rejected.

In Rwanda, and all over the world, stone foundations in different forms have been the norm for permanent buildings for centuries, from rubble foundations to mortared ones to plinths. My formal education in structural engineering in the UK did not teach me how to design with stone, but of course I learned how to design with concrete, which—for all intents and purposes—is reconstituted stone. In practice, it is quite common to find older buildings in the UK with stone foundations, and these foundations have kept the building standing for hundreds of years. When you think about it, stone is the perfect material for most foundation options—durable and strong. Traditional mortared stone foundations are a time-tested, local alternative.

Stone is readily available close to the surface. The local technique to remove large boulders is the same one that humans have been using for millennia—to heat and cool weaknesses in the rock, causing expansion and splitting. Large-scale geological mapping for the site was not available, so we studied maps published by the Royal Museum for Central Africa in 1981 and by the Rwanda Geological Service in 1991, which show the solid geology in relation to the site boundary and local features including the two lakes.

The 1991 map provides the most differentiation, but both show the western part of the site underlain by granitic rocks and the eastern side by metamorphic rocks including schists, quartzites, and metasediments. Due to the geologically long exposure of the bedrock to the tropical climate, it weathers through chemical decomposition to different grades of soil (residual soil) and weaker rock mixtures (saprolite).

The maps do not identify residual soil and saprolite thickness, but we were able to determine on our own that it varies across the site, and we also noticed that the composition of the soils reflects the sedimentary parent rock strata below. These strong, permeable soils that are not susceptible to movement allowed the use of stone foundations. At RICA, the quartzite stone was quarried from within ten miles of the site and we placed each stone individually into an interlocking pattern with others, and everything was caringly mortared by hand. We also included reinforced concrete grade beam to tie the foundation together and address any bending forces resulting from seismic activity.

The interlocking pattern is a guide, and it relies on the skilled masons with engineering supervision to follow the intent of the requirements with the material available. This technique was new to most of the masons, and they ended up nicknaming the interlocking stones after one of our structural engineers, Shakira Nyiratuza. The "Shakira Stone" approach ensures that the layers are interlocked. To build with stone is to work with what endures— not only physically, but ecologically. This foundation solution also reduced the project's embodied carbon by 60 percent compared to fully reinforced concrete solutions.

**Foundations for
the Future**

**by
James Kitchin**

The vertical bond stones
(the key to RICA's
interlocking foundation
system) were nicknamed the
"Shakira Stone" by workers,
in honor of structural
engineer Shakira Nyiratuza.

RICA's foundations include
quartzite stone that has been
interlocked, layered, and
mortared by hand, as well
as reinforced with concrete
grade beams to mitigate
seismic activity, which is
common in Rwanda.

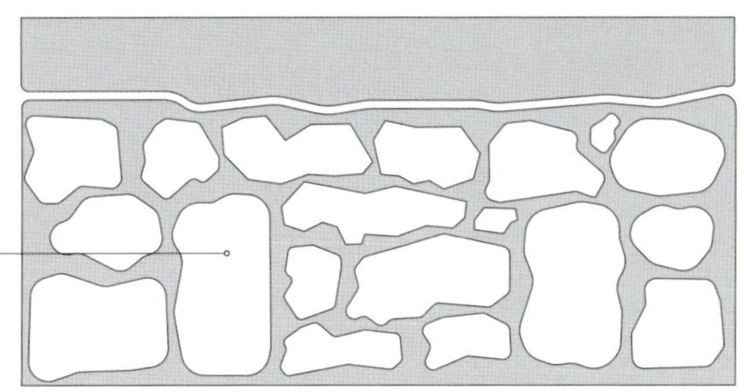

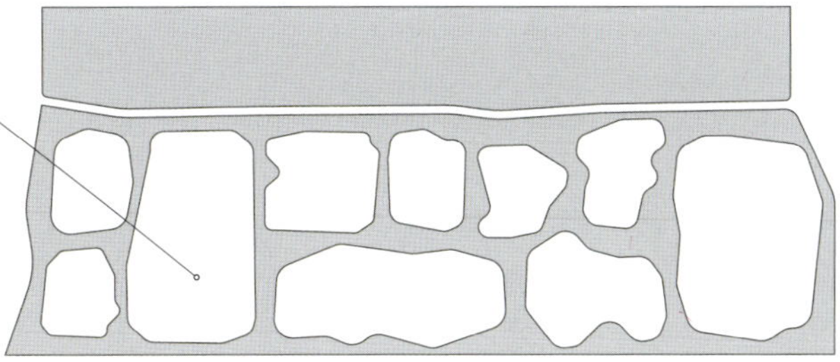

Earth is a common building material throughout the world and 90 percent of people in Rwanda live in earth homes today. Unfortunately, these buildings are often poorly built and use of the material was banned in the building code as a result. Yet, it is a building material with many potential benefits. Regionally, the type of soil known as laterite is plentiful and its attributes make it excellent for construction. It is cost-effective and can easily be installed by the same masons accustomed to working with brick or other masonry units. The thermal mass and hygrothermal properties buffer heat and humidity, ensuring a comfortable indoor environment. Finally, the environmental impacts of the material, including embodied carbon, offer a significant reduction from most other construction materials. For these reasons, we pursued earth as the predominant walling material for the campus.

We estimated we needed thirteen thousand cubic meters of soil to make 2.5 million compressed earth blocks for the campus. We evaluated different locations to source the soil from the site to minimize the impact on the ecology and productive farmland. The four chosen sites represented different soil types that were tested for their properties to make structural building materials. Ultimately, we sourced from an existing "borrow pit" on the site, which is less than five kilometers from the main portion of the campus.

Well before any buildings were designed, we collected large volumes of the soil to mix with lime or cement stabilizers (or sometimes with each other) and manufactured the material into compressed earth blocks or rammed earth cylinders. We then performed laboratory testing on those cylinders to understand the characteristics of each soil mix with regards to strength and durability, which helped us identify the ideal source and mix.

During this design-stage feasibility study, we made and tested over two hundred samples to find the ideal mixes and, in doing so, we became familiar with the behavior of the soils in a way that could not be represented in numbers. After months of working with the soils we were able to identify by sight and touch when they had reached their optimal moisture content, which is correlated to strength.

Without careful design and knowledge of the materials, the earth walls are vulnerable to erosion from heavy rainfall. The buildings are designed with a "good hat and boots," meaning significant roof overhangs and a base layer of fired bricks, to protect them from driven rain, ground water, and splash back. In addition to this, an earth plaster protects the block walls and can be repaired and maintained over time. Through this material, we are introducing a culture of care for our buildings.

The relationship of seismic-induced moments and permanent axial force in the walls dictates the reinforcement requirements for the earth walls. This relationship is a balancing act. A higher permanent load means the walls can resist a higher moment. However, increasing the permanent load causes larger seismic forces, leading to larger moments in the walls. This led to regular-shaped buildings, which minimize recesses and extrusions on plan, to ensure even and predictably loaded shear walls. Longer walls, four meters and greater, are prioritized because they are more effective than shorter walls that added up to the same total length at resisting the overturning moment because the reinforcement in them has a longer lever arm from the center of the wall.

MASS was asked to build upon their experience in earth construction, structural and geotechnical engineering, and research capacity to work with the government as part of a consortium to revise the building code and incorporate safe, effective earth standards. Along with the Rwanda Housing Authority and the Rwanda Standards Board, MASS worked with EarthEnable, Rwanda Polytechnic, and Greenpact Africa to demonstrate that earth can be safe, durable, and affordable. MASS created two important documents based on RICA's lessons, including "RS 484: Adobe blocks (Rukarakara)—Specification" and "Technical Guidelines on Adobe Block Construction in Rwanda." Both are written in English and Kinyarwanda to be accessible to the typical home builder, and both include low-tech tests that have been correlated with scientific laboratory testing.

How to Repurpose Soil for Walls

by
James Kitchin & Rosie Goldrick

Compressed Stabilized Earth Block

Recipe:

1 Move and store topsoil to one side
2. Excavate soil below the organic layer
3. Sieve and remove any aggregate larger than
   seven millimeters in size
4. Combine with a pre-blended cement pozzolana
5. Mix: 5 percent in the dry season and 7 percent
   in the rainy season to increase durability
6. Add water to achieve the optimum moisture content
7. Manually compress into a brick form
8. Store and cure for twenty-eight days protected
   from rain and direct sunlight

MASS continues to support the Rwandan government in the implementation and dissemination of these documents, working towards the continued and safer use of a familiar material in Rwanda. Not only is it good for the local economy, but it's also good for local ecologies. Compared to using fired brick, a typical adobe home saves 2.9 tons of upfront greenhouse gas emissions, as well as avoiding air pollution and deforestation. Paired with guidance to improve safety and durability, these homes are projected to be longer lasting, resulting in additional environmental benefits. When finally the adobe blocks come to their end of use, they can return to the ground—a perfect circular product.

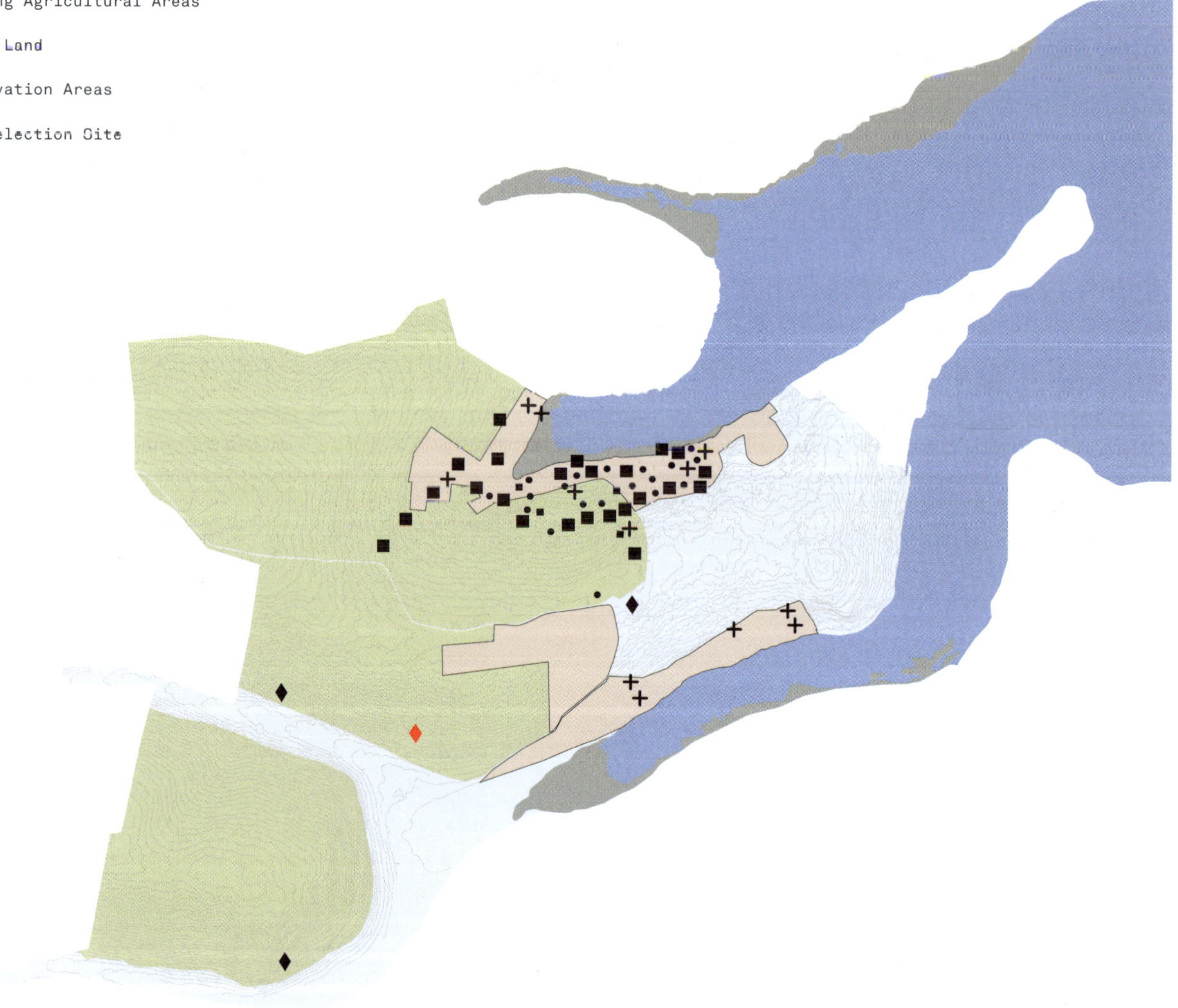

Savannah Woodland

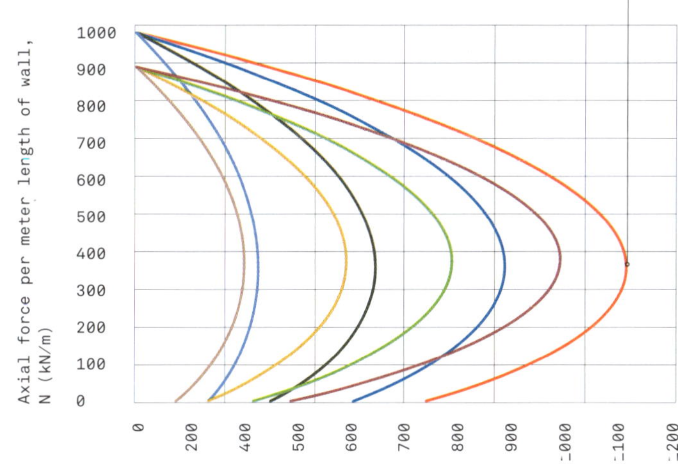

N-M interaction curves for 240 mm-thick
CSEB walls of varying length and provided
reinforcement

2 m wall, B16@500 (blue)
2 m wall, B12@500 (red)
4 m wall, B16@500 (gray)
4 m wall, B12@500 (yellow)
6 m wall, B16@500 (green)
6 m wall, B12@500 (brown)
8 m wall, B16@500 (orange)
8 m wall, B12@500 (dark blue)

Clay is a material of intense complexity and contradiction. It's rough yet refined, humble yet elevated, dirty yet pure. It endures temperatures that would destroy most other materials and emerges transformed.

Clay in the form of terra-cotta and ceramics plays a significant role in craft and construction in Rwanda. Ceramic tableware is common throughout the country, much of which uses naturally occurring dyes for the glaze composition. Because of its traditional uses, and our desire to elevate and add value to existing economies, we featured this material in a variety of ways throughout the campus.

For use as a wall and floor tile in kitchens and laundry areas we worked with Wellaris Ndongozi and his team at Webo Ceramics. Pendant lights and wall sconces incorporated hand-thrown fixtures produced by Gatagara Cooperative, and all of the buildings are sheathed in clay roof tiles manufactured by Ruliba Clays Ltd.

Ruliba Clays is the largest producer of terra-cotta building products in the country. Their clay is sourced from various quarries in Rwanda and their kilns fired with waste from agricultural processes, primarily using discarded coffee husks. Working with Ruliba and their equipment supplier, MASS developed a custom form for use in Rwanda. It can be used for both roofing and wall cladding, while also internally managing water flow, and reducing the total weight of clay. The MASS team worked closely with the team at Ruliba to monitor production and kiln durations of the new product and ensure consistent deliveries to the building sites. This evolved into the development of an Environmental Product Declaration, the first of its kind in Rwanda, which tracked their production from start to finish.

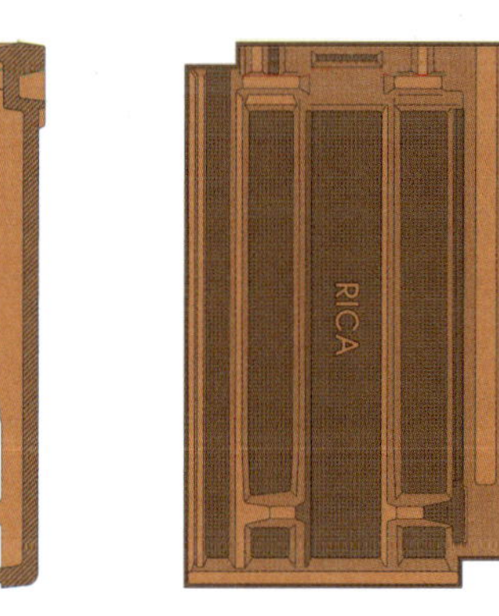

Earth Elevated to Craft

by **Chris Hardy & James Kitchin**

Savannah Woodland

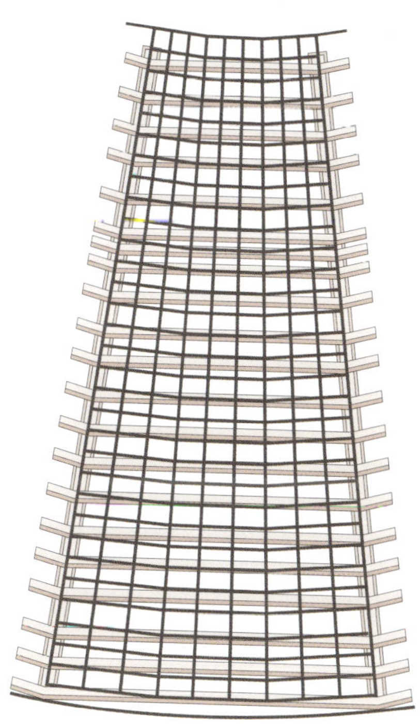

To control warping during kiln firing, the mass of each kiln car had to be balanced.

The battens of Year 2 and 3 roofs are arranged radially to create a smooth curvature in the tiles.

Left: Wellaris Ndongozi,
founder of Webo Ceramics
Right: Efurem Rusumbabahizi,
potter for Gatagara

In the early months of the RICA project, we spent a significant amount of time researching and mapping the networks of materials suppliers and craftspeople in the region and across the broader country. Ultimately, this became a network of eighty-five artisans, weavers, ceramists, metalworkers, and woodworkers across Rwanda that we engaged during the project. The aim was to replace imported furniture by sourcing local materials and seeking out traditional handcraft techniques to create beautiful, durable, repairable, and sustainable products. The details for the design of the furniture were inspired by the traditional craftsmanship, culture, and heritage of Rwanda and by the end, we had designed over 250 different products. We designed every single object, including the toilet paper holders, the wardrobes, the beds, academic furniture, the chairs, tables, hooks on the wall, and the door handles on the cabinets.

There's a third thing that is as important as form and function when thinking about furniture—the signature of the artisans, a recognizable handprint of their craft. Instead of a wooden backrest for one of our chairs, we made a woven backrest produced from traditional Rwandan sisal basketry weaving. For our conference tables, the edges were hand-carved by a wood-carver. Details like this make the furniture special, but they also make RICA's furniture the literal signatures of its artisans. We developed a model where we combine traditional techniques and locally sourced materials to produce beautiful, resilient, and sustainable products as an alternative to imported products. This model also supported the makers on different levels. Besides creating opportunities to upscale their quality and access to training, we generated enough work to support the makers over the longer term with a stable income stream. We worked collaboratively with the artisans to refine and iterate on designs to understand how to best utilize the inherent qualities of their materials and methods. These handmade pieces reflect the reality that human creativity and natural materials can coevolve in balance.

**Forging a
Purpose-Built
and Handmade
Future**

**by
Niels Datema**

From left to right:
Uwimana Joseli
Aline
Nsabarushimana Oreste
Akimana Clementine
Niyogisubizo Perajiya
Clementine
Devotha
Muramira
Kemushabongo Eric

Eighty-five artisans, weavers, ceramists, metal
and woodworkers across Rwanda worked to make
furniture for RICA—carving wood, dyeing fabric,
weaving grasses, and finishing the pieces that
included every possible object you'd expect to
find in a school. For RICA's furniture, MASS used
the native species *Markhamia lutea* (umusave),
which can be harvested without machinery
by hand.

Savannah Woodland

Savannah Woodland

MASS has adapted our practice, expanded our disciplines, and maximized the positive impact for our partners and the communities they serve. In the years preceding the work at RICA, we expanded from our roles as architects to include engineers, landscape architects, furniture designers, filmmakers, storytellers, and, of course, builders.

Every project starts with building trust and cultivating relationships. Since our founding, we have stewarded partnerships and human-centered design grounded in "accompaniment," a model of engagement we learned from Dr. Paul Farmer, co-founder of the international nonprofit health organization Partners in Health. From the beginning, MASS saw the project not simply as an opportunity to design a climate-positive university, but to extend our values into the act of building itself.

RICA was an opportunity for MASS to design the full process—from curriculum and campus planning through to buildings, landscape, and furniture, down to the construction itself. Before a single drawing was complete, our team was on-site. We walked the land with ecologists, met with local craftspeople, tested soils with our hands, and sat with students, teachers, and mothers to understand their hopes for the campus. These early conversations informed every design move, but they also shaped how we would build.

We knew that building in this region came with challenges: limited infrastructure, remote access, and a history of extractive construction practices. But it also came with opportunity: skilled artisans, deep material knowledge, and a strong culture of collective work. The goal was not only to construct buildings that reflected these values—but to create a process that could strengthen them.

We got to work on research of the building materials long before a building was drawn. There were many early morning hikes through the savannah looking out for new flora and fauna.

Our team made compressed earth blocks on the future site and tested them. We rooted through the markets in Kigali looking for hardware. We hired a fisherman to help us conduct a survey of the lake bed. We dug into the rate of kiln drying of roof tiles. We ensured that the buildings could be built with the skills of the local labor and the materials that came from the site. In the simplest sense, we asked what more could we do to make the design as impactful as possible.

The team responded to submittals and answered requests for information, challenging contractors to follow the procedures we had outlined in our drawings and specifications: to report to us on local hiring, diesel fuel consumed, and the percentage of female workers on-site. There were eight MASS employees on-site at the time, across several disciplines. We witnessed craft improving among our workers, and we could see the savannah thriving next door. We could hear the piercing calls of African fish eagles from the tops of protected trees within the construction site.

Midway through construction, the global pandemic struck. The original contractor, facing mounting obstacles, stepped away from the project. At that moment, MASS made an unprecedented decision: to take over construction directly. To keep the momentum of the project going, we hired 1,300 of their staff and took over construction of the project.

The campus is made of stone, earth, timber, and clay—but it is also made of hands. Over 90 percent of the workforce came from the surrounding Bugesera District. More than three hundred artisans were trained in weaving, furniture making, rammed earth construction, and finish carpentry.

There's a story behind every door handle and truss joint. One carpenter, trained through the project, now leads a team building new schools across the region. A group of weavers who created furniture for the student housing have since launched a cooperative. These legacies were never an afterthought—they were part of the design.

Our colleague, and architect on-site at RICA, Jean Paul Uzabakiriho, summarized it well in saying, "We would rather struggle to find the best solutions for this project than become complacent and default to what is typical." Construction can, and should, be different. It can be designed as a force for good in the same way that we approach our design work.

A Model of Construction

by
Chris Hardy

Architecture today is in a state of flux, responding to an ever-changing world marked by a growing climate crisis and an increasingly unjust global order. More than just the act of building, architecture is undergoing profound transformation. It is shifting, expanding into new fields, and retreating from others as it grapples with the present. In this state of crisis, conversations about architecture often begin with an acknowledgment of the urgency of our times—particularly the climate emergency. Architects and related professionals must diversify their approaches, remain adaptable, and take responsibility for the damage we have historically caused.

The global crisis, largely driven by the development of the built environment and its heavy reliance on technological advancements, presents a paradox. However, the systems that have exacerbated our challenges may also hold the keys to addressing them, provided they are employed wisely. This moment in history demands that architecture, traditionally focused on construction, must now engage with broader social, economic, and ecological systems that both influence and are influenced by it.

Recent architectural practices recognize that past models are inadequate for addressing contemporary needs. MASS, from its inception, has distanced itself from conventional architectural practices, academia, and professional norms. In doing so, MASS has embraced an approach rooted in immediacy—responding directly to the pressing needs of communities, particularly in the Global South. Through its work, MASS frequently rediscovers knowledge that has been long dismissed or devalued. This knowledge, often rooted in traditional wisdom, is increasingly relevant today. MASS's work integrates these principles with contemporary strategies, creating a bridge between past and present.

At the intersection of architecture, community development, and material supply chains, these projects reimagine construction as a business model that prioritizes social impact and ecological balance over profit maximization. The success of these initiatives is not measured by traditional architectural excellence but by their ability to reshape the relationship between space, society, and sustainability. This evolving practice has the potential to redefine architectural practice itself.

Metronomic Practice: From Despair to Possibility

by Hanif Kara, OBE

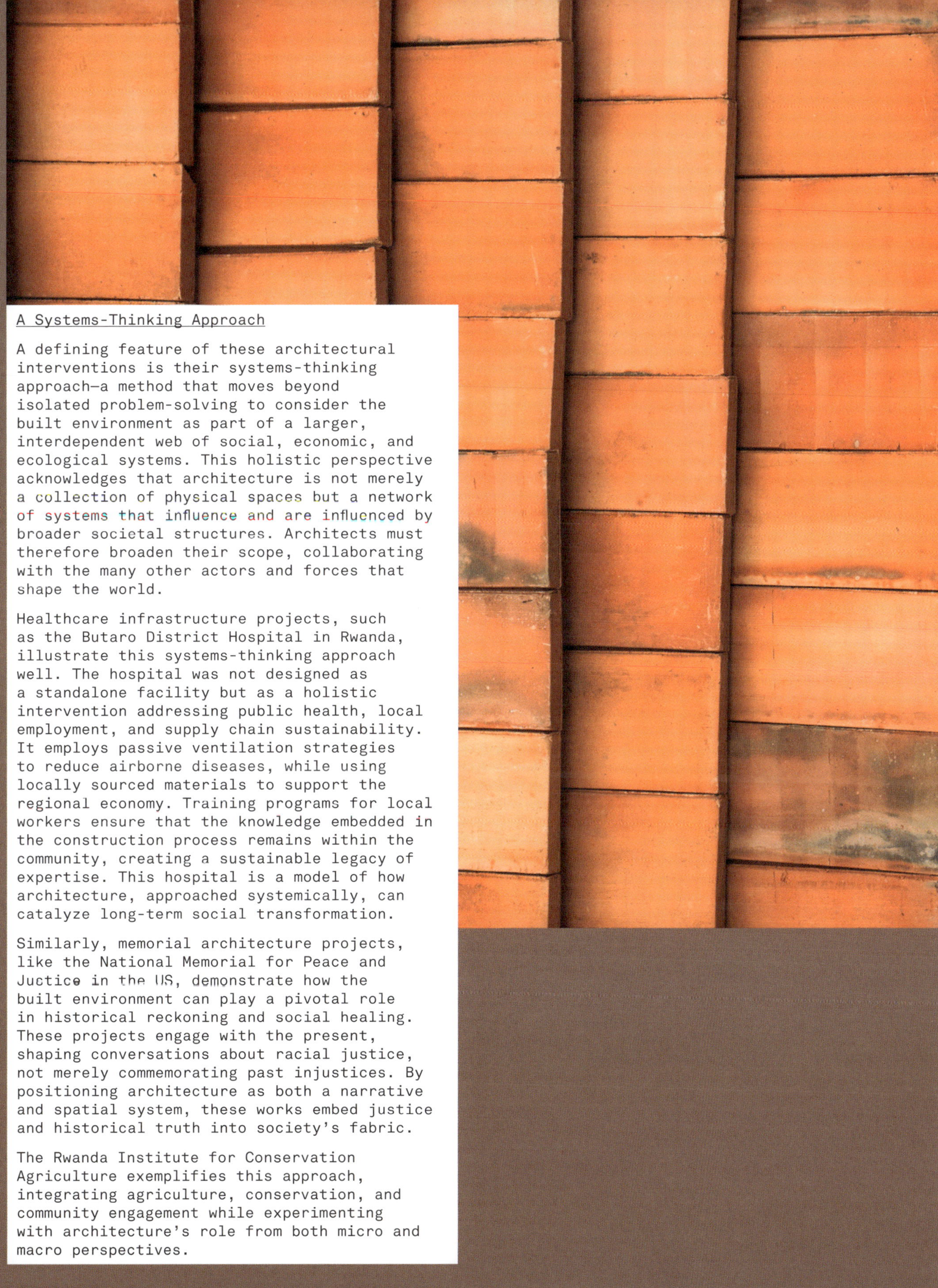

A Systems-Thinking Approach

A defining feature of these architectural interventions is their systems-thinking approach—a method that moves beyond isolated problem-solving to consider the built environment as part of a larger, interdependent web of social, economic, and ecological systems. This holistic perspective acknowledges that architecture is not merely a collection of physical spaces but a network of systems that influence and are influenced by broader societal structures. Architects must therefore broaden their scope, collaborating with the many other actors and forces that shape the world.

Healthcare infrastructure projects, such as the Butaro District Hospital in Rwanda, illustrate this systems-thinking approach well. The hospital was not designed as a standalone facility but as a holistic intervention addressing public health, local employment, and supply chain sustainability. It employs passive ventilation strategies to reduce airborne diseases, while using locally sourced materials to support the regional economy. Training programs for local workers ensure that the knowledge embedded in the construction process remains within the community, creating a sustainable legacy of expertise. This hospital is a model of how architecture, approached systemically, can catalyze long-term social transformation.

Similarly, memorial architecture projects, like the National Memorial for Peace and Justice in the US, demonstrate how the built environment can play a pivotal role in historical reckoning and social healing. These projects engage with the present, shaping conversations about racial justice, not merely commemorating past injustices. By positioning architecture as both a narrative and spatial system, these works embed justice and historical truth into society's fabric.

The Rwanda Institute for Conservation Agriculture exemplifies this approach, integrating agriculture, conservation, and community engagement while experimenting with architecture's role from both micro and macro perspectives.

Craft, Technology, Knowledge, and Being

Adopting an epistemological lens—one that examines the nature of knowledge—reveals how these projects synthesize craft and technology. The integration of both is not merely aesthetic but a strategic decision that enhances both quality and functionality while fostering community engagement. The architectural strategies we observe in these works combine cutting-edge technologies with traditional craft techniques, creating innovative structures that are contextually grounded. This ensures the architecture remains sensitive to local culture and history, responding to future needs while honoring the past.

By embracing local craftsmanship, these projects recognize the tacit knowledge embedded within communities—insights often overlooked in conventional architectural practices. This aligns with the concept of "epistemologies of making," where construction is seen not just as a technical process but as a knowledge-producing activity. Engaging local artisans is not only a means of preserving cultural heritage but also a way of infusing projects with unique, place-specific qualities that standardized, industrialized construction methods may lack. Additionally, technology serves to enhance, rather than replace, the human touch in these projects.

An ontological perspective—examining the nature of being—adds another vital dimension to these architectural works. Architecture, through an ontological lens, is not merely a structure but an agent of being, shaping how people experience the world and themselves. It challenges the traditional notion of buildings as static entities and views them as dynamic environments that influence how individuals interact with one another and the world around them.

From this ontological perspective, architecture becomes an intimate expression of human experience. It influences the way we relate to one another and to space itself. The architecture of these projects is a medium through which communities negotiate their identities, histories, and futures. By integrating an ontological understanding, architecture shapes not only the functional aspects of space but also the emotional and psychological impacts on its inhabitants.

This approach encourages architects to consider how buildings make people feel— whether they foster connection or alienation, belonging or exclusion. It calls attention to the sensory and experiential qualities of architecture, such as the interplay of light and shadow, the texture of materials, and the arrangement of space, which can profoundly affect human consciousness. Architecture, from this perspective, is a site of being, not just of shelter.

Through both epistemology and ontology, architecture bridges the gap between knowledge and experience. Knowledge is not just abstract but embodied and lived. This integrated approach allows architectural practice to become more holistic, more human-centered— recognizing that architecture is not just about what we know, but about how we feel, how we exist, and how we connect with the world and each other.

Redefining Architectural Practice

Ultimately, this body of work calls for a redefinition of architectural practice—one that resists the traditional separation between architect and community, between design and impact. These projects exemplify an emerging model of architectural agency that is participatory, ethical, and embedded in systems thinking. Rather than viewing architecture as a finite act of construction, these projects see it as an ongoing process of engagement, learning, and adaptation. Architecture becomes a conversation between space, society, and the environment.

The examples discussed here illustrate how architecture, when approached with systems thinking, epistemological insight, and a craft-centered lens, can contribute to a more equitable and sustainable future. This approach embraces complexity and difference, rather than simplifying or homogenizing, and redefines what architecture can be in response to contemporary crises.

By integrating systems thinking, technological innovation, and traditional knowledge, these projects not only respond to immediate challenges but also reimagine the future of architecture as a discipline deeply embedded within broader societal, ecological, and economic networks. In doing so, they offer a model of practice that restructures the systems that create problems in the first place.

Architecture as an Adaptive System

In a world increasingly defined by uncertainty—due to climate change, social upheaval, or economic instability—these architectural projects demonstrate that architecture must be adaptive, responsive, and deeply integrated within its surrounding systems. These interventions do not impose rigid solutions but develop context-specific responses that evolve with the needs of the people they serve. Rather than offering a universal model, the approach creates a flexible framework that adapts to different circumstances over time.

For instance, research into climate-resilient products and sustainable material sourcing challenges traditional construction methods that prioritize efficiency over ecological responsibility. Sustainability is not treated as an afterthought but embedded into the design process. This approach aligns with regenerative design principles, which not only minimize harm but create buildings that actively contribute to environmental and social well-being. Adaptive architecture provides a nuanced and responsive model for addressing the challenges of the twenty-first century.

Hanif Kara, OBE, is a practicing structural engineer and professor in practice of architectural technology at the Harvard Graduate School of Design.

As part of the Fashion for All concept, Cedric Mizero created in December 2017 the exhibition and art installation *Strong Women,* which featured photography, fashion, and mixed media highlighting feminine strength, energy, and responsibility.

This work intended to showcase and give voice to the rural women of Rwanda and recognize and appreciate women's strengths and role in the society. Cedric designed the Fashion for All exhibition to raise awareness of societal issues, and to be a voice for people through artistic expresssion.

Strong Women, Celebrating Farming and Farmers as Something Aspirational, Dignified, and Beautiful

by Cedric Mizero

Savannah Woodland

Afromontane
Forest
Fossey

The Dian Fossey Gorilla Fund supports gorilla conservation and education in Rwanda. Located in Volcanoes National Park, the twelve-acre campus reflects the Fossey Fund's mission to advance conservation as a complex, collective commitment to endangered species and future generations. MASS designed the campus to foster biodiversity and resilience by propagating plant and native species and regenerating the land. The goal of the project, as well as the foundation, is to foster a passion in all visitors for conservation principles in this living laboratory.

Gorillas are beautiful, resilient animals. They are
our closest living relatives, sharing 98 percent of
our DNA. Just like humans, they form bonds that
last a lifetime, they wean their children, and they
mourn their dead. They contribute to—and benefit
from—communities that are social, supportive,
and vital to their survival. Thanks to the Fossey
Fund, and others like it in the region, the mountain
gorilla population went from critically endangered
to endangered—numbering over one thousand.
But, it is a fragile victory, and their home in the
Volcanoes National Park sits right on the edge
of the tension between conservation and human
settlement. This tension will continue to create, for
the foreseeable future, a critical need to amplify
awareness around the importance of the Fossey
Fund's mission.

**Advancing the
Legacy of a Lifetime of
Conservation Activism**

The Fossey Gorilla Fund was founded fifty-
five years ago by Dian Fossey, the legendary
primatologist, and is the world's largest and
longest-running organization fully dedicated
to gorilla conservation. Fossey galvanized a
generation of conservationists through her
fieldwork, extensive research, and tireless
advocacy. The campus provides more than a
home for that mission. It provides an infrastructure
for local, regional, and global communities to
advance conservation principles. In its design
and construction, it embodies the regenerative
principle that abundance is found in the balance
of thriving human and ecological systems.

In her final journal entry before being
murdered in her tent at the Karisoke Research
center, Dian wrote, "When you realize the
value of all life, you dwell less on what is past
and concentrate on the preservation of the
future." The campus honors Fossey's legacy by
fostering sustainable practices and inspiring
future generations to continue her critical
work in protecting endangered species.
This campus provides a living tribute to her
lifelong commitment to gorillas by intertwining
conservation and education, and by growing the
efforts of the local community, the Fossey Fund,
and conservationists worldwide to preserve
our shared future.

A conversation about partnership,
capacity building for Rwanda, and
staying focused on conservation
principles at the Fossey Fund's
new campus.

PG   Our first conversation and
relationship with the Fossey Gorilla Fund
started in 2017 around a simple idea to create
a new campus for the organization in Rwanda.
However, through conversations and workshops
with the Fossey Fund's team, the idea grew into
a much bolder vision and mission to use this
project as a catalyst to inspire people to
commit to a lifetime of conservation activism.
The clarity and solidarity around this vision
became a driving force for all of the decisions
for the campus, from the site selection on
what had been agricultural land at the base
of the Virunga Mountains; to the programming
to support research, education, and community
initiatives; to the design of the buildings;
and to the construction methods. Every person
who participated in or touched the design and
construction of the campus carried that mission
forward. From the start, the project asked how
conservation can be more than protection, and
how it can become a generator of opportunity,
resilience, and balance.

EG   The clarity in the project's mission
and goals is what led MASS to believe that we
could start a construction company to build
this project, and the Fossey Fund to agree
that this was the best option for achieving
impact. This belief also guided us through a
lot of unpredictable situations as we started
construction during COVID and even during
some of the tough conversations and decisions
we had to make along the way in terms of
value engineering and costs of construction
escalating. I felt that through it all we were
aligned as partners, accompanying the Fossey
Fund on this journey.

Regenerating
Lost Landscapes
and Ecologies

TG   We were able to translate the mission
of creating conservation activism into a
physical, tangible place that illustrates the
unique methodologies to make participation
accessible. Just as Dian Fossey pioneered
conservation work in this region and shared
it with the world, we sought to embody that
same ethos through the design, to test, learn
and share what is happening on this campus
with others. We've since seen this thinking
proliferate in relation to the national park
expansion planning and regional effort to expand
regeneration. Beyond the day-to-day activities
that the Fossey Fund is doing, the campus is
showing how to restore and regenerate land for
conservation. It demonstrates a new model of
community-based conservation.

TS   We ended up getting this wonderful
lead gift from a donor, from Ellen DeGeneres
and Portia de Rossi, that really elevated
the project in a lot of ways. It was really
important to me that this project had an impact
while we were building it, and I say that from
the perspective of leading the organization and
my team, but also from the perspective of the
donors that were involved. That's what MASS
really brought to the table and it really opened
my eyes to the amount of impact we could have,
not only for our team to have a purpose-built
home but through the process of building it.

TG   This alignment between mission
and method reflects the deeper goal of the
campus: to create a space where the values of
conservation and care are embedded in every
layer, from process to place. The mission for
this project led to one of the boldest examples
of what system-scale change can look like in a
project—and the Fossey Fund was such a dream
partner in that endeavor. The way that we were
able to shape the fundamental vision around
large-scale thinking of conservation, implement
it at a site level, and then carry it forward to
regional impact is really unique.

EG   The decision-making on Fossey was
really rooted in our goals for larger impact
beyond the project—beyond the campus. How
the design process unfolded led to other
opportunities to think about new ways to do
things, or to take a chance and think about what
it might mean for MASS to build this project in
Rwanda. Capacity-building was a big part of this
project for the Fossey Fund's future plans.

TU   We saw building capacity as critical
to the community's interests, too. On a lot of
the construction sites, you may not be able to
even put together a group of women because it's
just a few of them who are typically allowed
to be there. But the fact that 20 percent
of the workforce on this project were women
in construction, in administration, and in
leadership is a huge win for this project and
for Rwanda.

EG   This construction site felt, at
least for me, very different to any other
construction site I had been on because there
was intentionality around equity and around a
larger goal to have women in leadership roles on
the project, building from the legacy of Dian
Fossey. There was this shared understanding
that you are following in the footsteps of
groundbreaking women in their own fields who
paved the way for others, and a shared feeling
that you can do this and we're in this together.

TU   In terms of building capacity, I think
another big win was to actually materialize a
training program that would certify or give
people the opportunity to showcase or to prove
that they've developed the skills. We trained
workers on every MASS construction site before
Fossey, and here we had the opportunity to work
with an organization that understands what a
community's livelihood means, as well as the
opportunity to work with the local polytechnic
university to certify the training program.
So we've been able to train about six hundred
people on the construction site, which you're
unlikely to be able to achieve on another
construction site. But also, to be able to hire
six hundred more people was a big community
collaboration with local leaders—people who have
skills that we need and people who need the
jobs. It creates balance

TS   Before MASS, we were working out of
a house in a town twenty-five kilometers away,
then it was two houses. Then we went into an
office building. We had one meeting room for
four hundred undergraduates every single year.
In fact, we had one meeting room for all our
staff work, as well. We were on a main busy
road, and we had a stadium behind us. So, if
there was any event going on, you couldn't hear
yourself think. We'd done things like convert a
kitchen into a lab just to get by. So, in our
mind, we really just wanted a space to do our
work—including the work of outreach. We had
seven thousand visitors in our old facility the
year before COVID hit. In the last three years,
we've had one hundred thousand visitors come
through the campus, and half of them have been
Rwandans, which is important because we really
didn't have Rwandans visiting us before unless
we brought them to the campus for work.

TG   The ability to regenerate lost
landscapes or ecologies is something that there
are not as many precedents for. It became
a conversation around how you think about
regeneration in a way that is not being done in
this region, and that will be an important part
of conservation and restoration moving forward.
It has been incredible to see it realized.
There were a lot of times we asked, "Can we
actually do this?" Sustainability is an all-
encompassing word that gave us a lot of options
and we carefully approached all of the site
systems, from the way that water is managed,
to habitat creation, to the way that education
is embedded. All of this became one narrative
about whole-systems design. Planting on this
project really stands out strongly as one of the
major points of collaboration and innovation,
especially within our team and the way that it
connects into the conservation narrative.

TS   When people think of campuses, they
think of built space—and when I tell the story
of Fossey, I'm always like, "Well, yes, we have
these three big buildings, and we have the
two dorms, and then we have this whole other
'building' of the campus—the landscape itself,"
whose creation required as much if not more
consideration than the architecture.

TG   Propagating the scale of native
plants needed for the campus was a huge
effort to pursue and something that hadn't
been done. It required a lot of research and
knowledge and a willingness to try. The ability
to do conservation at a really big scale
and regenerate existing ecologies is still
something that needs additional exploration
and understanding.

TU   Beyond the technical or the design
thinking, the relationships we built on this
campus, and continue to build, and the education
or knowledge-sharing we've been able to
facilitate has for me, personally, connected me
to this opportunity to learn about conservation.
It's a world that most architects will not have
the chance to necessarily know. But then when it
comes to design, of course, and as an architect,
I have had an opportunity to think about what
regeneration means at small scales and at big
scales.

TG   At the onset there was just a bit of
questioning and uncertainty about what a site of
this scale could achieve; what is realistic when
you compare it to something that's really huge,
like a national park. This size of effort does
have a real impact that is valuable because,
as a society, we still do not appreciate how
rapidly we have degraded our land. To begin to
restore it means that every scale of effort
matters and that even the smallest interventions
can have a really meaningful impact.

PG   Globally, it is hard for people to
know where to start. It's also hard for people
to know how to act differently and if they do
succeed in acting differently, as Therese has
mentioned, measuring if their small actions are
actually having potentially larger impacts.
And I think one of the amazing lessons of this
project is the protagonist in this whole story,
which is the gorilla, and the deep connection
people forge with gorillas, whether they're
emotionally connected to them, or nostalgically
connected through Dian Fossey, or scientifically
connected because of their research. The
goal of this project was to leverage those
connections as the entry point to engage more
deeply in conservation.

EG   Part of this was really setting it up from the beginning to be able to build this sort of narrative and empathy journey that takes you on this path of understanding and feeling embedded in the work that Dian did. Then, for us, it was about wanting to build empathy for conservation and build empathy for gorillas and our connection to gorillas—empathy for their plight—and about wanting to inspire others to act and be advocates for the conservation world.

TS   I'll just add one other thing, too. I think we think of it a lot within the context of Rwanda locally, in the area adjacent to the park, and its impact, but also on the country. What's been really exciting for me to see is we've hosted trainings now that have had early career conservationists from more than thirty different countries, from South America, Europe, Asia, Africa—and having a place where these folks can come together and talk about these really critical issues and the similarities that they may see in their landscapes to other landscapes, to build a network together. We have the ecological protection science side of what we do, and then we have the very big human side. Ultimately, conservation is about people because of what's happening to the planet. And our two areas of focus are training and providing opportunities for early career conservationists and working with and partnering with local communities to address basic needs. I would've never in a million years thought that building a campus could so directly touch on this core part of our mission.

TU   I was on the Fossey campus just last week—stepping out of the architect's role to see what the project brings to people, not only the communities around the campus, but also all the visitors that come through. Building this campus offered a sense of ownership and purpose to the people who built it, and a connection to the story of Dian and the work that the organization is doing. If you talk about modern conservation, it's about Dian's legacy on behalf of the gorillas, but in that legacy, you can also see the faces of our colleagues and the community members who championed this course of action.

Patricia Gruits
Co-Executive Director, MASS

Emily Goldenberg
Design Director, MASS

Therese Graf
Design Director, MASS

Dr. Tara Stoinski
President, CEO, & Chief Scientific Officer,
Fossey Gorilla Fund

Theo Uwayezu
Design Director, MASS

The Fossey Fund's campus sits on agricultural land that had been heavily degraded after years of cultivation and is directly adjacent to the national park where Fossey and, later, the Fossey Fund's team worked to protect the gorillas and conduct research. MASS's vision for the campus focused on regenerating the land as a living laboratory—a place that would demonstrate climate adaptation, biodiversity restoration, and resilience. By exploring the five nearby volcano mountain ecologies, MASS developed a plan to propagate and plant native species. As a laboratory, the campus is a test bed for reforestation methods that can influence both local and regional efforts to create better biodiversity. As an educational center, the campus is a beacon for other conservation organizations hoping to restore balance within the ecosystems they monitor and protect.

Rob and Melani Walton
Education Center

Cindy Broder
Conservation Gallery

Sandy and Harold Price
Research Center

**Galvanizing
a Legacy for
the Fossey
Gorilla Fund**

Afromontane Forest

Each year, the Fossey Fund equips many students and budding researchers with immersive training in conservation science, research techniques, and effective science communication. Conservationists and school groups alike explore the Fossey Fund's campus—open each day of the year—which is composed of the Sandy and Harold Price Research Center, the Cindy Broder Conservation Gallery, and the Rob and Melani Walton Education Center. The central atria of each building, about ten kilometers from Dian's Karisoke Research Camp, admit clerestory lighting and mimic her original cabin nestled in the forest. MASS devised a plan to propagate native flora in the landscape around the buildings, making it both an educational campus and a living laboratory.

Trails throughout the Fossey Fund's campus offer students and researchers alike an interactive way to understand the balance necessary within ecosystems. The Gorilla Trail allows visitors to walk through the forest as if they were living the daily life of a gorilla, learning about their movements, diet, and behavior. The Biodiversity Trail highlights the different ecologies of the Volcanoes National Park, providing a window into the richness and fragility of the region's plant life. The Wetland Trail demonstrates how natural systems, such as wetlands, can treat wastewater sustainably, filtering the water back into the environment and replenishing resources.

Afromontane Forest

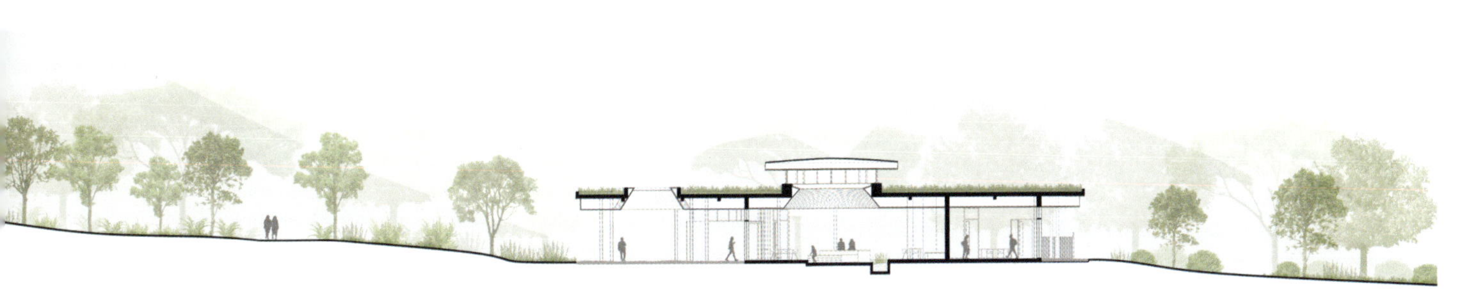

Afromontane Forest

Karisoke Scientific Forum

Afromontane Forest

Cindy Broder Conservation Gallery
1.   Entrance
2.   Exhibition hall
3.   Outdoor exhibition
     and reading area
4.   Theater
5.   Gorilla café
     and gift shop
6.   Outdoor gathering space
     and café seating

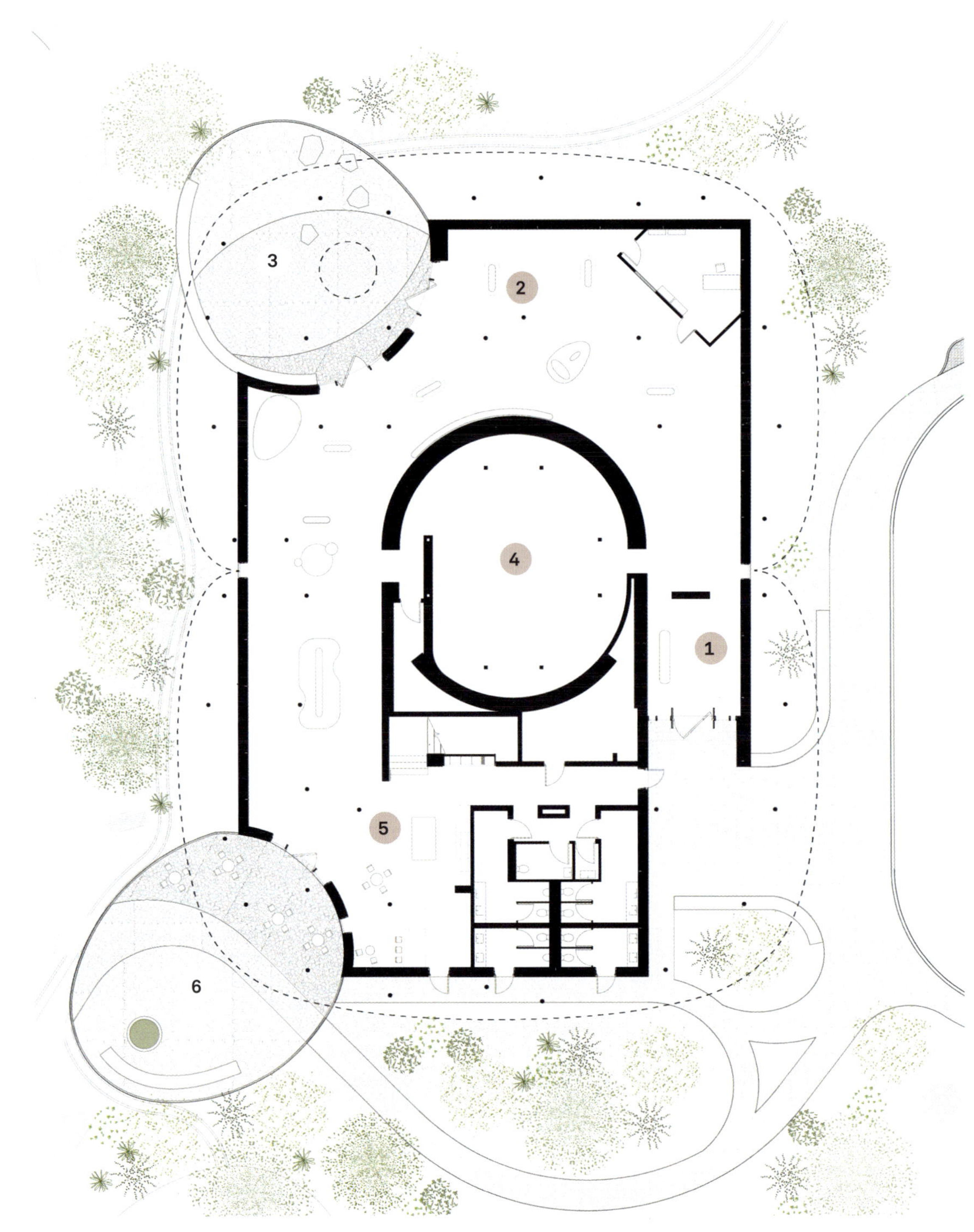

The Cindy Broder Conservation Gallery at the Fossey Fund's campus is a public-facing space welcoming international tourists, students, scientists, and local Rwandans, which offers an in-depth look into the life and legacy of Dian Fossey, the gorillas she studied, their habitat, and the impact of human activity on their survival. For the Fossey Fund, it was essential to create an educational environment that tells the story of gorilla habitat conservation, fostering scientific understanding of them as a species and their broader needs and environment. Working with the Fossey Fund, MASS developed a set of core messages and experiences for the visitors, to inspire lifelong conservation activism through empathy.

The approach to exhibition design was inspired by Dian Fossey's method of "breaking the boundary," the process of habituation through which she gradually gained the trust of gorillas. MASS sought to guide visitors through a gradual transformation from observer to engaged participant. The exhibition unfolds in three key chapters: "Dian's World," "Gorillas and You," and "Modern Conservation." Within each chapter, there were specific immersive and multimodal storytelling opportunities to honor Dian Fossey's legacy and share the rich stories of mountain gorillas. Through materiality, design motifs, and interactive components, the exhibition is crafted to cultivate empathy, forge connections, and inspire action. Natural and local materials, including Rwandan wood, were used throughout the exhibit.

The exhibit begins with "Dian's World," a series of dense, hanging scrim banners surrounded by immersive photomurals, which recreates Dian's cabin where she lived in the Virunga Mountains for many years. The denseness of this first space eases as visitors begin to understand the gorillas, their habitats, and their behaviors. For "Gorillas and You," MASS mapped out an experiential arc throughout the entire gallery space, meant to move visitors from curiosity to understanding, then to engagement and inspiration, and finally, to empowerment.

The final chapter of the exhibition "Modern Conservation" highlights the people working on the front lines of conservation for gorillas today. Designed as an active space for discovery, it invites visitors to step into the roles of tracker, scientist, or community activist. The broader goal of this section is to leave visitors with a deeper understanding that conservation is a complex, community-driven effort—and that they, too, can play a role. The exhibition experience extends beyond the classroom—the whole campus serves as an educational tool. An extensive "living laboratory" on the former agricultural site includes more than 250,000 native plants dispersed across the campus and interpretive trails, creating a regenerative landscape that brings biodiversity back to this former agricultural space and provides unique educational and research opportunities.

Conservation as Empathy

by
Maggie Stern & Bethel Abate

Gorillas and You
Ingagi nawe
Lending a
Helping Hand

The landscape team believed that reusing the local lava stone available on-site not only for the buildings, but also to define a continuous ground plane intuitively, was essential. The lava stone paths ground the body on a local material, shifting the scale, finish, and pattern of the stones to communicate transitions and facilitate easy circulation, while also allowing for water infiltration and integration with planting. Large hexagonal lava stones are stacked into site walls, cut into slabs for terrace pavers, and crushed into aggregate for site trails.

The pebble-shaped terraces cantilever over the landscape or cut into wild gardens, creating an array of experiences that range from private and quiet meeting spaces to active and welcoming entry plazas flanked by stone seat walls. The ground transitions from a singular, taut surface to a gradient of pavers and aggregate that extends to meet reforestation gardens and draws plants inward amidst the joints. The paving is a design layer that tells a material story about edges, blurring, reciprocity, and balance.

Dian Fossey's research was driven by her willingness to accept the animals on their terms, to never push them beyond the various levels of tolerance they were willing to give. "Any observer," she said, "is an intruder in the domain of a wild animal and must remember that the rights of that animal supersede human interests."

Observation, patience, and time allowed Dian to gain the acceptance of the gorillas. Imitation and "aping" (scratching, facial grimacing, munching celery, copying vocalizations, deep belching, and knuckle walking), a term she used to describe her actions when actively observing the gorillas, drew the gorillas close to her and she used their natural curiosity in her habituation process. Dian's vulnerability and participatory approach profoundly influenced the campus design—the curvilinear dance of path experiences, the interpretive trail themes, the myriad pebble-shaped gathering spaces that connect interior and exterior, are located to take advantage of striking views to the volcanoes in the distance.

These intentional and layered design moves create interactive, immersive, and reciprocal moments between the visitor, student, or researcher and the birds, pollinators, and living landscape.

Dian's methods of observation and her research about gorilla movements and behavior are implicit in the materials, movement, scale, interpretive trails, and ecology of the landscape. Powerful pieces of her story and her invaluable research have been designed as spatial experiences for visitors, integral to the way the campus was designed and organized. Blurring boundaries between human/gorilla, national park/agrarian field, and research/education was an early design question. How can the campus design erase the hard edge between two habitats and design around the idea of collaborative prosperity? How can the campus be a managed and rewilded landscape at the seam between protected and productive landscapes?

Answering these questions through the design required careful consideration of the unique needs of both sides—the critical needs of the communities living near gorillas (food security, fuel, clean water, livelihoods) and a deeper understanding of how these needs put pressure on the gorillas' forest home (poaching, deforestation, encroachment, water harvesting).

**Finding Reciprocal
Patterns in the
Landscape**

**by
Maura Rockcastle**

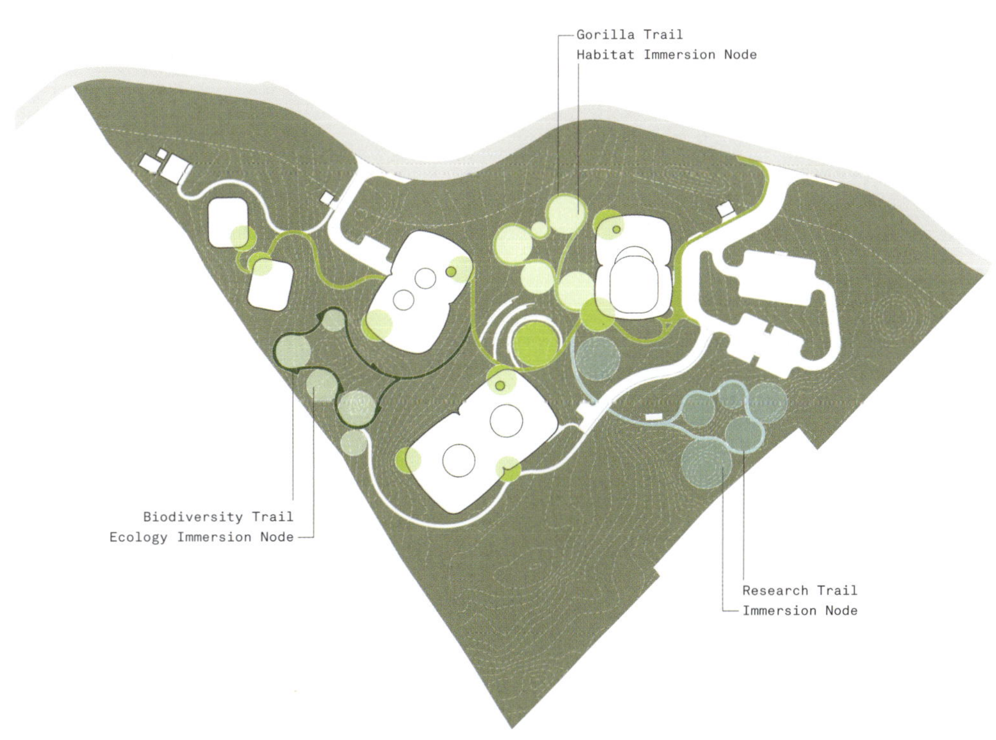

Gorilla Trail
Habitat Immersion Node
Biodiversity Trail
Ecology Immersion Node
Research Trail
Immersion Node

Afromontane Forest **Case Studies**

Reclaiming and Restoring
Lost Ecologies

Water Is a Resource

Refining Construction as
Social Infrastructure

Considerations of Working
with Volcanic Stone

Dignity Through Design

Gaining Capacity Through
Filmmaking

Measuring Abundance for
People and Planet

Tracking Landscape Restoration
and Plant Propagation

From the very beginning of this project, the landscape team was thrilled to collaborate with scientists who shared our passion for plants, ecologies, and landscape systems. The team conducted comprehensive research on the biodiversity found within Volcanoes National Park, creating a detailed list of native species. This was meticulously reviewed by Fossey's scientists to identify and refine the selection list of ecologically strategic framework species and initiate succession within each ecotype. Framework species selected for restoration projects are typically fast-growing and hardy; they provide shade and shelter, improve soil and microclimate conditions, and facilitate biodiversity by attracting animals and supporting seed dispersal. Using this curated selection of species, MASS developed a planting design tailored to the site's unique environment, the objectives of the Fossey Fund's education programming, and the goal of testing various approaches to forest restoration. Few of these species were commercially available, so careful planning for sourcing and propagation was essential to achieve the necessary diversity, quality, and quantity of plant material—while also creating opportunities for training and market development.

Guided by the expertise of the site team, over three hundred thousand native plants were propagated and planted, contributing significantly to the restoration and preservation of the park's natural habitat. This thoughtful process of selecting, sourcing, and cultivating native species on a formerly degraded site exemplifies our belief that abundance arises not from excess but from care, knowledge, and regeneration. The sourcing phase was a year-long endeavor that required close collaboration with the local community. MASS provided detailed information and images of the 120 native species selected for the planting design, helping community members to search for these species locally. They began their search within the construction site's boundaries, gradually expanding to neighboring agricultural land, and adjacent to the Virunga National Park's vicinity.

For species that no longer existed outside the park's boundaries in the project's area, sourcing extended to other regions of the country. Botanists from the Fossey Fund also provided support during this process, offering insights into the natural habitats and growing conditions of hard-to-find species, and guiding the community to likely locations. The language barrier was another challenge faced during this phase of the project, as the local community knew the plants by their local names, while our plant list had scientific Latin and common English names. To bridge this gap, community members would bring samples of the species they identified. Our team then reviewed and identified the correct specimens for sourcing.

On-site, propagation began simultaneously with sourcing, managed by our dedicated nursery team. Due to the delicate nature of these species, propagation was initiated within two days of sourcing to maximize growth success rates. Many of the native species are not well documented in terms of their propagation methods. As a result, the nursery team experimented with various techniques on the first batch to identify the most effective methods. Daily propagation numbers were recorded, revealing a high initial propagation rate but lower success rates for growth.

The planting phase was the most efficient, completed within three to six months. As soon as construction zones became available, MASS commenced planting immediately, ensuring no time was wasted. The nursery team continued to maintain the newly planted areas for the following year, carefully nurturing the plants to maximize success rates. The process of research, sourcing, propagation, planting, and subsequent monitoring established a foundation for several ongoing initiatives. It served as the first restoration trial in anticipation of the future national park expansion. Through continued monitoring, the Fossey Fund team authored an academic paper on the potential of framework planting to enhance biodiversity within eighteen months of installation. The planting also enabled them to conduct on-campus testing of five distinct ecosystems,

Reclaiming and Restoring Lost Ecologies

by

Joe Christa Giraso

providing a practical teaching environment for monitoring forests, wetlands, and other ecological systems. This continues to contribute to a deeper understanding of the long-term sustainability and ecological dynamics of Volcanoes National Park, particularly in the face of climate change. This learning curve highlighted the importance of patience in propagation, as well as shaded structures and adaptive practices. After planting, botanists from the Fossey Fund periodically visited the nursery to monitor plant development.

"We had hoped that this landscape could highlight the value and the beauty of native species and plants, those that we can also find in [the] neighboring Volcanoes National Park. We also wish[ed] that this landscape could serve a multitude of functions and purposes: engaging visitors & tourists that come here, educating students, local or higher education universities, showcasing model approaches to reforestation, sustainability with green roofs, and serve our scientific program as well, all while also being aesthetically pleasing.

I remember at the very beginning when we were asked to compile a list of some species we would like to see here [on campus]. Deo and I and some others in the biodiversity team came up with a list of over 130 species. We were positively shocked a few months later when we got a question—of the list you gave us, there are four or five that we have trouble allocating and growing on-site. That means you managed to get all the other hundred plus. That was something we never expected would be possible here.

We created this amazing place that sets an example of what one can build if you have a heart for conservation in general, and also conservation of local species, local plants, local insects, and a drive to be sustainable. The mindset is to merge knowledge from across disciplines, where science can also come into architecture and into design, and then receive and give feedback throughout this whole process."

—Yntze van der Hoek, biodiversity expert for The Fossey Fund (2018–23)

Left to right: *Hypericum revolutum, Polyscias fulva, Cynoglossum amplifolium, Dryopteris pentheri, Macaranga capensis, Carapa grandiflora, Impatiens burtonii, Pycnostachys goetzenii, Carduus nyassanus, Neoboutonia macrocalyx, Plagiochila colorans*

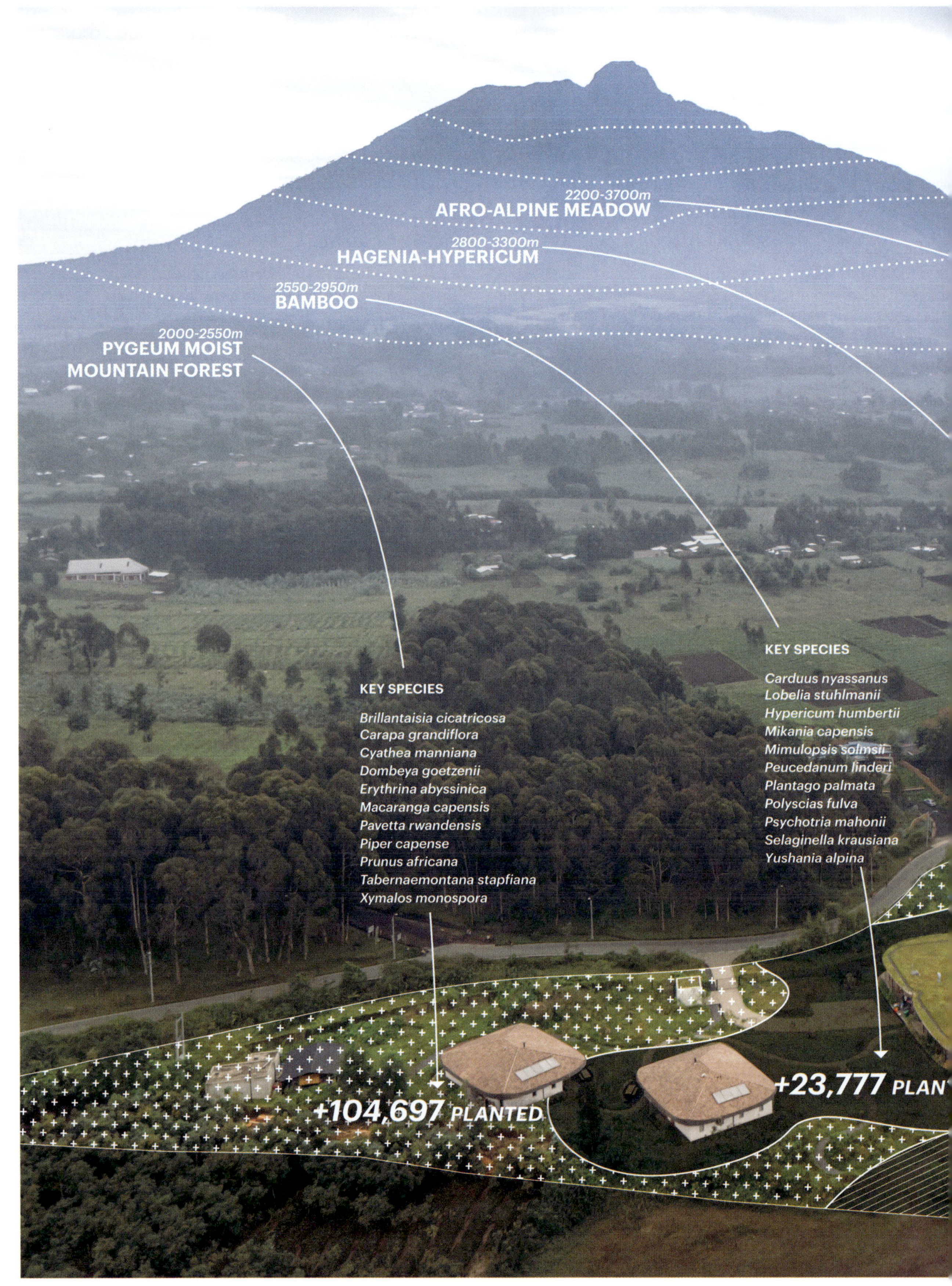
2200-3700m
AFRO-ALPINE MEADOW
2800-3300m
HAGENIA-HYPERICUM
2550-2950m
BAMBOO
2000-2550m
PYGEUM MOIST
MOUNTAIN FOREST
KEY SPECIES
Brillantaisia cicatricosa
Carapa grandiflora
Cyathea manniana
Dombeya goetzenii
Erythrina abyssinica
Macaranga capensis
Pavetta rwandensis
Piper capense
Prunus africana
Tabernaemontana stapfiana
Xymalos monospora
KEY SPECIES
Carduus nyassanus
Lobelia stuhlmanii
Hypericum humbertii
Mikania capensis
Mimulopsis solmsii
Peucedanum linderi
Plantago palmata
Polyscias fulva
Psychotria mahonii
Selaginella krausiana
Yushania alpina
+104,697 PLANTED
+23,777 PLAN

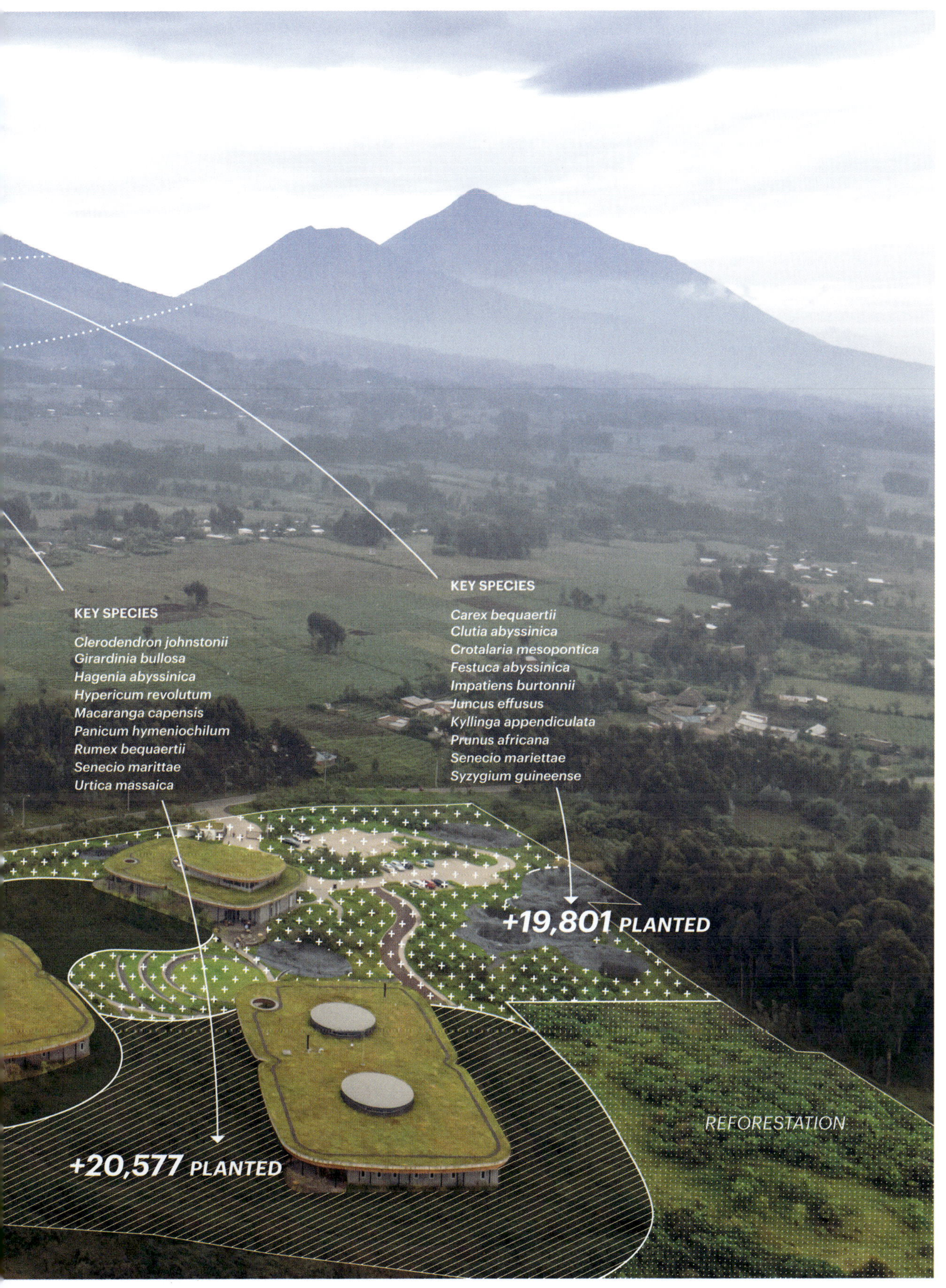
KEY SPECIES

Clerodendron johnstonii
Girardinia bullosa
Hagenia abyssinica
Hypericum revolutum
Macaranga capensis
Panicum hymeniochilum
Rumex bequaertii
Senecio marittae
Urtica massaica

KEY SPECIES

Carex bequaertii
Clutia abyssinica
Crotalaria mesopontica
Festuca abyssinica
Impatiens burtonnii
Juncus effusus
Kyllinga appendiculata
Prunus africana
Senecio mariettae
Syzygium guineense

+19,801 PLANTED

+20,577 PLANTED

REFORESTATION

MASS believed that water management should be approached holistically as an integral part of the design and as an experiential element of the site. This is a sharp departure from common attitudes in this region, which see water either as part of a natural system or as something highly engineered, used, and disposed. Regionally, there are few examples that demonstrate how water can be intentionally integrated as a vital resource— one that is valued, sustainably managed, treated through natural systems, effectively recycled and reused, and ultimately recharged into the local aquifer. But, the Fossey Fund's campus is unique in how it manages all types of water, from stormwater to gray water to wastewater, using design strategies tailored to each source.

Stormwater from oversight flows and buildings is directed through the landscape in a series of naturalized channels, swales, and ponds to create localized capture that increases the rate of retention and reduces the risk of negative impacts that could compound downstream. The educational trails throughout the campus demonstrate the inextricable relationship between water and the plant communities that depend upon it. Gray water from the buildings is captured and reused within the building, resulting in a reduced overall demand of other sources for toilets and irrigation. Wastewater is collected from each building and directed towards a centralized wastewater treatment wetland, which is the first of its kind in the country. Composed of an anaerobic baffled reactor and a series of naturalized wetlands, the system filters waste incrementally through planting medium, which absorbs nutrients and breaks down waste before release into papyrus mulch basins that offer final absorption and infiltration.

This approach demonstrates how water can be celebrated through design, managed with natural systems, collected to create habitats, and made an element of education. Water, once seen as a linear resource, becomes cyclical, symbolic of the regenerative systems this project hopes to inspire elsewhere.

**Water Is
a Resource**

**by
Therese Graf**

2.
3.
4.
5.
6.
7.

The scale of the Fossey Fund campus required MASS to build out a construction division, managing resource allocation and maximizing the project's social, environmental, and economic benefits. MASS tailored an assessment framework for both project-specific goals and broader indirect effects, including environmental sustainability, education, equity, economic growth, and emotional well-being to track impact. This development brought substantial economic opportunities to the communities surrounding Volcanoes National Park, with over 2,400 individuals employed during construction.

To equip workers with essential skills, MASS collaborated with the German Corporation for International Cooperation (GIZ) and the Integrated Polytechnic Regional College in Musanze (IPRC Musanze), offering specialized training in masonry, carpentry, steel fixing, electrical work, plumbing, health and safety, and green roof installation. We were able to prove that it is possible to efficiently deliver high-quality construction outcomes and achieve lasting environmental and social impacts for the community and the world.

MASS continued to identify critical gaps in the built-environment ecosystem. We found that, despite making great efforts during the design process to embed our philosophy and principles into the design of each project, much of the intended impact was at risk during implementation. This was due to several factors, including limitations in the availability of construction materials, technical skills, and equipment, as well as budget constraints. However, the most significant factor was that the construction companies operating in Rwanda did not necessarily share our objectives. They operated in a resource-constrained market in which they competed against one another to offer the lowest bids to win work, but once secured, they had to find any possible way to reduce costs. MASS hypothesized that, through a design-build approach, we could substantially reduce our time and effort trying to hold contractors to carry out

the design as intended and redirect that effort toward constructive problem-solving and the pursuit of the intended impact. During the final stages of construction, a team of seasoned experts came on to the project to finish the last pieces.

The construction team worked closely with the design team in the development of the drawing details to consider material selection, sequencing, sourcing, assembly, staging, and availability of skills. This dramatically reduced the need for further clarification during construction and allowed for efficient construction planning. The design team remained heavily involved during the construction phase, with several of the design team members based on the site full-time, actively participating in the management and direction of the construction activities.

MASS only subcontracted specific scopes and worked closely with subcontractors to integrate effectively into our design-build process. Whenever issues arose during the construction, our fully integrated team was able to quickly develop solutions, working with our in-house quantity surveying and procurement team to ensure the proposed solution's success. This holistic way of working allowed MASS to focus on sourcing materials with consideration, not only for their cost but also for their embodied carbon footprint. It allowed us to work in partnership with local community representatives to employ members of families who were in the greatest need of economic opportunity. With the support of GIZ and the Government of Rwanda, we were able to train and certify over six hundred of the workers who participated in the construction of the project in a trade such as carpentry, metalwork, and masonry. Importantly, we were able to deploy international industry practices for construction health and safety, including the use of quality personal-protective equipment, secure scaffolding, and appropriate measures for working at height and for high-risk activities such as welding and using heavy machinery and other power tools.

Refining Construction as Social Infrastructure

by

Martine Dushime & Adam Saltzman

Among the 2,400 individuals employed by MASS, 23 percent were women—an achievement in the construction industry globally and certainly in Rwanda. From Dian Fossey and her esteemed contemporaries Jane Goodall and Birutė Galdikas, to fifty-five years of the women-led Fossey Fund, to the leadership of the campus today, it's an achievement that is part of a larger legacy in this region. Female workers formed a cooperative to pool resources into a rainy day fund, securing a financial future for themselves and each other. They invested in a small potato seedling business, ensuring that when the project ended, they left the jobsite with earnings, savings, and future opportunities.

The cooperative also became a space for connection and support, where women could openly discuss challenges, celebrate achievements, and receive guidance from community leaders on topics such as health and sanitation. Many of these women also received formal training and certifications in trades like masonry, steel fixing, and carpentry through a partnership with MASS, GIZ, and IPRC Musanze, which will provide them and their families with new career opportunities for years to come. Through this project, women not only helped build a campus—they built stronger futures for themselves, their communities, and the next generation.

Located at the base of the Volcanoes National Park, the Fossey Fund's campus sits on fertile volcanic farmland formed from ancient lava flows, which inherently results in highly variable and unpredictable ground conditions. The five-acre site features a complex geological makeup, with layers of collapsible, loose granular soils often mixed with hard, porous volcanic stones, creating inconsistent soil conditions within the building footprint.

Despite comprehensive geotechnical investigations, the intricate nature of the volcanic terrain at the Fossey Fund's site made it almost impossible to foresee all potential challenges at hand. In certain areas, solid volcanic stone layers concealed caves or weaker soils below, leading to unsuitable formation material, which impacted excavation levels and required continuous foundation redesign to adapt to on-site conditions during construction. The presence of shallow hard rock also imposed significant difficulties that made excavation works particularly laborious. To reduce waste, a stone crusher was subsequently installed on-site to crush excavated hard rock into aggregates, which was used to make low-strength concrete, mass concrete, and hardcore to be used for a variety of works on-site.

Considerations of Working with Volcanic Stone

by Aimable Mukire

CINDY BRODER
CONSERVATION GALLERY

By repurposing as much local stone as possible, MASS not only reduced the need for imported materials but also celebrated the region's heritage.

The stone was used in the exterior cladding of buildings, while volcanic ash, a byproduct, was incorporated as a pozzolanic supplementary cementitious material—making it stronger and more durable, and significantly reducing the project's embodied carbon. This approach drew inspiration from our earlier use of volcanic stone at the Butaro District Hospital. There, skilled masons perfected the art of hand-cutting and laying stone with minimal mortar, a method that has since evolved and been passed down. Two of the original Butaro masons now lead their own cooperative, sharing their expertise and fostering a skilled local workforce.

MASS's philosophy emerged from years of hands-on experience and learning on construction sites around the globe. It serves as both a challenge and an invitation to reconsider the construction process as a vehicle for meaningful impact. It's focused on four core principles— hiring locally, sourcing regionally, training where possible, and, most importantly, viewing every design decision as an opportunity to invest in the dignity of the communities we serve.

Dignity Through Design　　**by Theo Uwayezu**

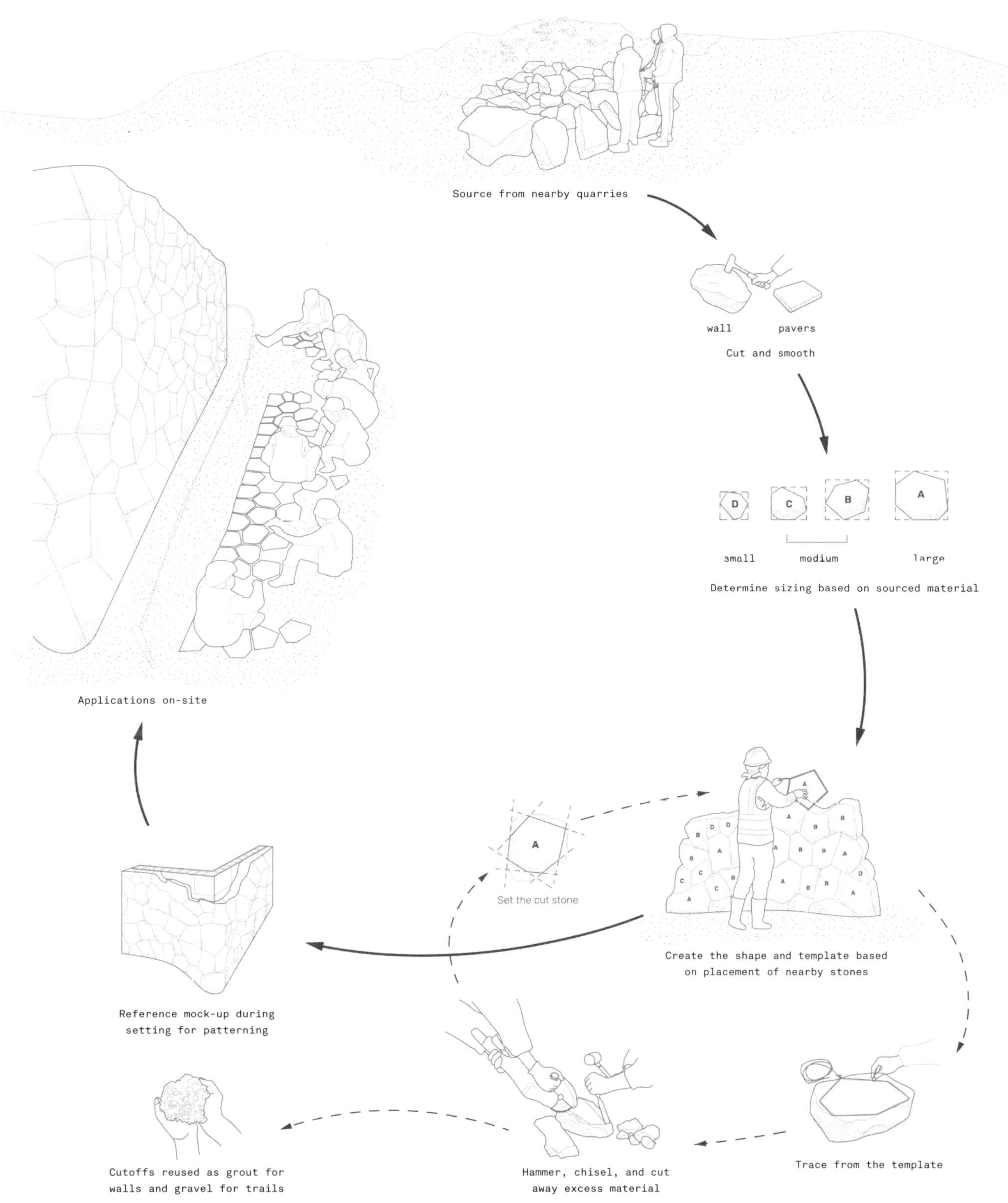
Source from nearby quarries
wall   pavers
Cut and smooth
D   C   B   A
small   medium   large
Determine sizing based on sourced material
Applications on-site
Set the cut stone
Create the shape and template based
on placement of nearby stones
Reference mock-up during
setting for patterning
Cutoffs reused as grout for
walls and gravel for trails
Hammer, chisel, and cut
away excess material
Trace from the template

One of the Fossey Fund's legacies is its ability to successfully and consistently bring the stories of mountain gorilla conservation and community impact to the world. MASS has been pairing film with architecture for over a decade as a mechanism to illustrate the breadth of the design and construction process and how it impacts individuals and communities, ecosystems, and even global policies. At the beginning of the campus project, we identified as a team an opportunity to pair our organization's storytelling and filmmaking capacities to expand the impact of the entire design and construction project. MASS established an in-house film team in Rwanda with the support of the Fossey Fund and the Ellen Fund to document and amplify the impact stories that grew out of the campus's design and construction.

Our filmmakers collectively spent over one hundred days on-site in Kinigi, interviewing, and filming with mountain gorillas, as well as with community members, government officials, construction and design team members, researchers, and park rangers. Throughout the project, that media was edited into videos, photos, and essays that illustrated and advocated for the impact the project was having. This allowed all the project partners to better understand what was happening at multiple levels of the project and leverage those stories towards ongoing support. The film team members who worked on this project collectively gained thousands of hours of conservation storytelling experience, and many of them have gone on to leverage their expanded skills on behalf of the Fossey Fund and multiple other conservation organizations in Rwanda and internationally.

Gaining Capacity Through Filmmaking

by **Thatcher Bean**

"The Ellen DeGeneres Campus represents a huge expansion of our teaching and laboratory spaces, enabling us to not just increase but transform our programs to study gorillas and their critical forest habitat and bring educational opportunities to early career African scientists and members of the local community."

—Felix Ndagijimana, director of Rwanda Programs, Fossey Gorilla Fund

How do we know if we've created a future where people and the planet can truly flourish? We must begin with an understanding of the adversarial relationship between humankind and ecology and the power of design to intervene.

In Rwanda's race to feed a rapidly growing population, its agricultural practices shifted away from nurturing and cultivating and instead toward degrading the land and crossing ecological boundaries—all less than a generation ago. In 2000, the Rwandan government began a campaign to curb the negative impacts of these practices and usher more of its populace into the middle income by shifting away from a dependence on an agrarian economy to knowledge-based work. Outlined in a document called "Vision 2020," they articulated two priority paths: grow the construction sector and invest in the development of secondary cities. Yet, in the time of the Anthropocene, these priorities risked further encroachment of human settlement on the gorilla habitat in Kinigi.

MASS needed to go beyond simply identifying an architecture that embodied ecological abundance: We needed to design a process that embedded safer, healthier, and more sustainable construction methodologies, while also contributing to lasting economic development within the local workforce. Blending these two goals, we asked ourselves: When workers were trained on-site, was that truly a path into a higher-paying vocation in construction and a move away from subsistence agriculture? Did we learn conservation methodologies and practices that were brought home? And how do you take those learnings and share them, so that they influence government priorities for the next generation?

At Fossey, we adapted our process because we learned from the past. We paired on-the-job training with theoretical training and partnered with the Integrated Polytechnic Regional College in Musanze (IPRC Musanze) to formalize that training via a certificate program.

We were able to invest in robust survey research over three data collection opportunities. One survey was conducted at the early stages of construction in 2020 and one near the end of the job in 2021. These two surveys used a convenience sample of individuals on-site and available to participate, resulting in 238 and 258 participants, respectively. The third was implemented in 2023, over a year after the project opened, for which we sought to interview fifty men and fifty women, with an even mix of individuals who did and did not receive training on-site. To the best of our knowledge, we believe the samples to be representative of the total population of workers.

We hired 98 percent of the 2,400 construction workers on the project from the Musanze District. While many (68 percent) had worked on a construction site previously, only about a third of them had been trained, and almost all (92 percent) had less than three years of experience in the industry. Together with GIZ and IPRC Musanze, we conducted evaluations of workers—certified workers who may have had the skills but not the formal training. After the campus opened, 98 percent of respondents reported that the training had helped them develop their technical skills and advance their careers, and 79 percent reported that training had aided them in obtaining a higher salary in their employment after the Fossey Fund construction project. Most tellingly, the boost in salary persisted even a year after the project opened its doors.

**Measuring
Abundance for
People and Planet**

**by
Regina Chen**

Women saw the highest relative growth from their baseline incomes to their jobs after Fossey (88 percent, with men reporting a 50 percent increase and youth reporting a 29 percent increase). By the final survey, 19 percent of respondents reported a sustained change in their economic standing, having moved up in categorization from "Extreme Working Poor." An additional 15 percent reported sustained movement into the "Middle Class" quartile.

Our process of working with communities—of using architecture to serve communities—needs to move beyond the building. This was our philosophy for the Ilima Primary School project, as well as our overall mission in Musanze and Bugesera—but to achieve the kind of positive impact MASS wants to make, this approach needs to be the way we build everywhere. Like agriculture, architecture as it is usually practiced is extractive. How will we truly know if our effort to invest in an alternative will have sustained impact without making the investment in measurement?

```
Final Impact Report
1.    Environment
      Native plants
      325,791 propagated*
      214,695 planted
      *This number is a high-level estimate
2.    Education
      530 site trainings
3.    Economy
      99% of all employees are Rwandan
4.    Economy
      $13.4M invested in Rwanda
5.    2,426 total people employed
6.    Equity
      23% of all employees are women
      24% of leadership roles are held by women
```

The Fossey Fund, researchers, and scientists have monitored the campus since its completion to create vital information about biodiversity enhancement and species evolution. Although there was some uncertainty at the beginning of the design process about the availability of native species to plant and propagate, nearly all of the saplings of selected native species performed well with a 95 percent survival rate into the second year after planting. This result provides a precedent and data source within the region that can be used to expand regeneration in the adjacent landscape and model methodologies for doing so.

In addition to the success of the native plant species, native fauna has also been observed on the campus, which indicates that the site is providing habitats after a relatively short time. The potential for small sites that have lost ecological integrity to provide habitats can be overlooked and misunderstood within the larger dialogue of conservation. The need for sites that demonstrate how biodiversity can be restored, even at the individual parcel level, is critical to expand efforts towards regeneration in landscapes that are highly fragmented and parceled.

Tracking Landscape Restoration and Plant Propagation

by Therese Graf

50% Canopy
20% Shrubs
10% Subspecies
20% Ground Cover
PF
AG
CG
XM
HA
PA
ML
NM
MC
CMe
TS
PR
3 plants/sq.m
Hay over planting
MIYAWAKI
10 m
MC
ML
DG
MC
NM
PR
PR
5 m
Clear understory
Nuclei of R8m
NUCLEATION

Species richness was measured through observation alongside pollinator community analysis and bio-acoustic recording. The increase of bird species found on-site is one demonstration of the expansion of biodiversity and habitat provision. Bird richness sampling observed fifty-two species on-site over a 573-day sampling period, which is a significant increase from the previous conditions and comparable agricultural parcels adjacent to the site. Some unique species, which are often restricted to the native habitats of Volcanoes National Park, have also been observed, such as Stuhlmann's sunbird, which indicates that the site is beginning to transition towards an ecology that resembles the intact ecological park conditions.

"We deem our case study of a purpose-driven inclusion of native plants in a previously human-dominated landscape to be a model that could be effective across Africa," wrote Fossey Fund researchers in their initial report. "After all, efforts to resolve the trade-off between nature and increasing human footprints should be global and have as much potential in Africa as elsewhere."

The data proves that even modest interventions, grounded in place and shaped by community, can ripple outward into profound ecological abundance.

It has often been said that landscape is a polysemic medium: It can communicate a multiplicity of meanings depending on who lives, visits, invests, exploits, or conserves it, for example. This idea was proposed long ago by scholars in different disciplines, which indeed proves the point, including geographers, landscape historians, social historians, and cultural historians. In every case, landscape, it is argued, can be, like a text, open to being "read" and interpreted. As the place where all of life unfolds, it registers the interaction between humans and their environment, including not only how they have adapted ingeniously to it, but how they have transformed it, exploited it, destroyed it, and recovered it. As such, it is subject to many types of research in the natural and social sciences, and increasingly so in this era of climate disruption. Most often, the polysemic essence of landscape is seen as its virtue, especially in the design disciplines, as it evolves into an increasingly interdisciplinary field. However, landscape as a medium or a practice can be seen as hermetic, unavailable, and incomprehensible to many, especially those who live in the Global South, that is, the majority world.

Polysemy and interdisciplinarity also beg the question of intentionality. Why this? Why now? Why here? Today, for true change that reverberates beyond the physical boundaries of the site of intervention, design has to declare clear intentions, and clear intentions demand specific questions, the two most consequential being for whom and how?

The work presented here is a record of a paradigm shift in landscape architecture, where the "for whom" demands a challenging and fundamental question: the how. It is challenging because to embed a designed landscape—with all its intentionality and artifice—into a social, economic, and political structure without the preceding institutional frameworks of governance and public funding is anything but a given. Like other MASS projects in Africa, to design and build a landscape in Rwanda has required the organization and establishment of all the elements that, although invisible in the sense of having no direct material or physical presence, are necessary to sustain a work of landscape architecture that is of global utility—the preservation of biodiversity.

As a landscape architect, I am interested in the expansive definition of design that emerges during these moments of paradigmatic shift in the discipline, when long-established modes of understanding and producing ideas become unsettled and blurry before they become clear again. By clear I mean not only transformed in their physical sense but reconfigured in a new order of priorities.

Designing for change does not involve a singular unified process. Instead, designing change operates across a field of actions—intervention into an ecological process, the production of botanical knowledge, the implementation of new technology—not only to produce the work more efficiently, but to see differently, and the various interfaces required for the social production of nature. What emerges from this process of discovery is a field of intersecting and overlapping epistemologies and ontologies, and from this comes a new way of working, one that is inseparable from the social, economic, and material structures and possibilities of the place, rather than being imposed onto it.

To Present the World Anew

by
Anita
Berrizbeitia

At Fossey, reciprocity diminishes the physical and conceptual separations between architecture and landscape, cultivated and wild, territory and site, human and nonhuman, laboratory and field. Reciprocity is not only about formal gestures that tie together inside and outside. Instead, it is dependent on structural relations that often begin with one or more large-scale decisions that forecast and support more visibly apparent local strategies. The combination of multiple strategies at different scales, for instance, a formal strategy at one scale with a site-specific one at another scale, supports reciprocal relationships between the different elements of the campus, the site, the people, the territory, and the wildlife to be cared for. This is necessarily less dependent on form, although it does not entirely negate it, and more particular to the contingencies of the program (research and biodiversity protection) and site (degraded agricultural land in need of regeneration).

There are a few kinds of recicprocity to observe generally, all of which the Fossey campus asks us to consider:

- Reciprocity between architecture and landscape: Both building and garden convey the same message, in this case, the environment, through the framing of visual connections between the volcano and the building.

- Reciprocity between campus landscape, as cultivated garden, and wild nature as found in the Volcanoes National Park.

- Reciprocity between humans and nonhumans: Codependency is key to the survival of species.

- Programmatic reciprocity: Moments of disciplinary expansion are characterized by "intensifying knowledge production." At Fossey, the laboratory and the field are part of the same form of knowledge production.

The world is now understanding that climate change is a global process with global consequences at every scale, but not all communities are affected equally. Some will bear the greater brunt of the impacts. This demands a completely new approach to design, one that replaces the methods of Western practices—based on efficiencies arrived at through technology—that are carbon-intensive and dictated by the protocols and methods of advanced capitalism, its regulations, policies, and economics. To create abundant futures is to create labor.

To think about landscape is to think about labor, not only in the ongoing cultivation that is necessary in the management of all landscapes over time, but in the training and development of new skill sets to be applied elsewhere in the community.

Anita Berrizbeitia is professor of landscape architecture at Harvard Graduate School of Design.

My restaurant, Mezza Malonga, is located on a
spit of land in the middle of Lake Ruhondo,
to the east of the Dian Fossey Foundation's
campus. It's where I started the Culinary
Innovation Village on seventeen acres where
we grow 134 different varieties of plants,
vegetables, and herbs. We also have a spice
and fermentation lab, apprentice programs, and
a cooking school adjacent to the restaurant
itself. The scope of my mission is, first
and foremost, to promote the amazing local
product that we have—and I've learned that
the more I train, the more creative I can be
with what we grow. It took me two years of
traveling to know more, and because my own
restaurant concept is focusing more on African
ingredients, I had to visit the different
countries in Africa. So, we have fifty-four
countries and I have visited more than forty-
eight of them. I cannot talk about something
that I don't know, and Africa is a huge
continent, and we have such food diversity.
We have a lot of tribes and cuisines and
cultures, and my job was to go to learn and
create something unique that is inspired by,
say, grandmother's cuisine that is the basis
of what I do. We also focus on promoting green
agriculture because we only have one earth.
I'm also creating a business for myself and
for the local economy—so, yes, that's what
this is all about for me: promoting, creating,
innovating, doing business, training people,
and creating job opportunities. We want to
inspire many people, not only in Africa,
but worldwide.

I think focusing on the curriculum that we
create and that many more people can use
worldwide is one of the things that we're
very proud of sharing. At the end of a day,
when we talk about architecture, it's like
an art. As a chef, I do the same sorts of
things. If I want to create a cake, I think
about everything, like the materials I use,
the products I use, the way they look, and
how food makes people feel. Architects and
chefs both like to make people happy. If
an architect's hotel is good, then people
come for the experience. The chef's goal is
the same—to create experiences. People are
traveling for food. People are traveling
for new experiences.

Learn, Create,
and Inspire

by
Dieuveil Malonga

Dieuveil Malonga is a chef, founder of
Culinary Innovation Village, and owner of Meza
Malonga, a culinary lab in Kigali.

Barbel from Ruhondo Lake

Ingredients

- [ ] 600 g barbel fillet
- [ ] Salt from Lake Rose, Senegal
- [ ] Djansan and pébè from Cameroon
- [ ] 1 fresh lime
- [ ] 1 soup spoon Algerian olive oil

Preparation

1. Clean and remove the skin of the fish and take the fillet out.
2. Chop the fillet into small pieces between 5 centimeters and 6 centimeters.
3. Marinate fish with lime and a pinch of salt from Lake Rose, Senegal, and djansan and pébè from Cameroon.
4. Grill fish with olive oil for about 1 minute per side.

Mango Rougail

Ingredients

- [ ] 2 mangoes
- [ ] 1 lime
- [ ] 1 chili
- [ ] 4 g coriander
- [ ] 10 g red onions
- [ ] 4 g basil
- [ ] A pinch of salt
- [ ] 1 soup spoon oil

Preparation
1. Clean all ingredients.
2. Chop mangoes, chili, and red onions into small cubes.
3. Finely chop coriander and basil.
4. Put everything in one bowl and add salt, oil, and lime juice to taste.

Avocado

Ingredients

- [ ] Musekera avocado
- [ ] 1 teaspoon moringa
- [ ] 1 soup spoon wild honey
- [ ] Garlic
- [ ] 5 g ginger
- [ ] A pinch of Penja pepper
- [ ] A pinch of salt
- [ ] 5 g basil

Preparation

1. Clean and remove the avocado seed and skin.
2. Put the avocado in a blender with all ingredients: moringa powder or fresh, wild honey, garlic, ginger, Penja pepper, salt, basil, and blend all together to your desired taste.

Shito

Ingredients

- [ ] 500 ml vegetable oil
- [ ] 3 red onions
- [ ] 8 garlic cloves finely chopped
- [ ] 8 guinea peppers
- [ ] Ginger
- [ ] Thyme
- [ ] 70 g black dried chili with seeds
- [ ] 100 ml chicken stock
- [ ] 50 g dried shrimp
- [ ] 50 g smoked fish powder
- [ ] Salt

Preparation

1. Put oil in a saucepan and when the oil gets hot, fry onions, black dried chili, and garlic together with dry shrimp and smoked fish powder.
2. After 3 or 4 minutes of frying, put chicken stock in the saucepan.
3. Add guinea pepper and salt.
4. Cook slowly at low heat for about 30 minutes.
5. Mix all in a blender.

Mango

Ingredients

- [ ] 1 mango

Preparation
1. Clean and peel the mango.
2. Cut the mango into big cubes.

Cucumber

Ingredients

- [ ] 2 cucumbers
- [ ] 2 teaspoons honey
- [ ] 3 limes
- [ ] 2 lemongrass pieces
- [ ] A pinch of salt
- [ ] 2 spoonfuls olive oil

Preparation

1. Clean and remove cucumber skin and seeds.
2. Make cucumber balls using a Parisian spoon or melon baller.
3. In one bowl, put honey, lime juice, olive oil, and crushed lemongrass and mix with cucumber balls.
4. Put the mixture in the fridge for 6 hours.
5. Take out cucumber balls from the container, and leave all other ingredients (they are only needed to marinate the cucumber).

Seeking implies motion—a refusal to settle for what is, in pursuit of finding what could be. This book is not a conclusion, but an invitation to consider the choices we have in building our collective future. The challenges are ever mounting and it is easy to be overwhelmed. But neither despair nor naive optimism is a strategy. Every decision, every act of design, is a chance to advance a more just and beautiful world. In that spirit, we have tried to show that abundance is not excess—it is balance.

We cannot afford to frame the future as a binary: apocalyptic collapse or restorative return. There are multiple futures and they are shaped by the choices we are making now. At MASS, we've long believed that design is a tool of healing, not just of bodies or building, but of systems, relationships, and ecologies. To seek abundance is to imagine and build a world rooted in balance: ecological balance, social cohesion, and reciprocal prosperity.

Landscape and architecture have always been inextricably intertwined in our work. Our buildings are part of an ecology that shapes where they stand, how they are made, and who they serve. Our landscapes are regenerative forces, the only element of our built world with the potential to increase biodiversity, sequester carbon, restore soil health, and support all beings. These projects have brought theories into form, measurable in performance and material consequence to the people that use them, having chosen through design to improve the balance of the ecosystems they operate within.

My early work on the High Line, while working with James Corner Field Operations, transformed urban infrastructure into public landscapes and revealed the power of reinterpreting place. But it was in Rwanda, in designing the Butaro District Hospital, where landscape meant health, climate, and livelihood, that I began to understand landscape not as context, but as source. Not just where or what we build, but how, with what, and for whom. That shift—from viewing landscape as backdrop, to understanding it as an agent, from surface to system, from design to ecology—has shaped our work ever since.

Butaro also revealed landscape as essential to a more expansive understanding of care. Our partner, founder of Partner in Health, Dr. Paul Farmer, often said, "The idea that some lives matter less is the root of all that is wrong in the world." When we extend this thinking to all forms of life and the systems that sustain them, so often treated as expendable, we begin to understand how profoundly destructive this mindset has been, and continues to be.

Paul offered "proofs of possibility" in challenging what he called the "failures of imagination" that too often lead us to accept partial, insufficient solutions to systemic harm. To confront the entwined crises of health, inequality, and climate, we must not only design for survival, but for flourishing—for all species, across generations. Dreaming big is not naive, but rather necessary.

Afterword

by
Sierra Bainbridge

The projects in this book are evolving proofs of possibility, each one expanding what we understand to be achievable. At the Ilima Primary School, we saw how a building could emerge entirely from its own landscape: every material locally sourced, every craft learned on site, each decision reinforcing both conservation and community and demonstrating how thoughtful design can regenerate local economies and ecologies at once. At RICA, we built on those lessons and scaled them across a forty-hectare campus and sixty-nine buildings, integrating agroecology and One Health principles to show that agriculture and biodiversity need not compete; they can thrive together, demonstrating that regenerative systems can shape not just a structure, but an entire institution. And at Fossey, we asked: How quickly can we repair what's been lost? In less than two years, we witnessed a tripling of biodiversity on land once degraded, evidence that abundance isn't theoretical, it's measurable, particularly when design aligns with living systems.

These principles influence all our work—at an entrepreneur incubator in Kigali, we applied the most earth gentle strategy of adaptive reuse of both existing building and landscape, as well as bringing these lessons to the Global North in repurposing underutilized manufacturing space as the headquarters of a historic and innovative environmental group in the Hudson Valley. And we continue to learn in new contexts as Indigenous perspectives of generational interspecies stewardship shape our projects and approach.

As a landscape architect, I have witnessed the interplay between the natural and constructed world, from infrastructural to territorial. Through these projects, I more deeply understand not only the landscape we create, as well as the landscapes we must conserve and restore, but critically, that the landscapes from which our materials come from must also be part of the calculus in all our design decisions. In that sense, landscapes are foundational to all of our work. They shape where and why we build, how we build, and what we build with. And this is true whether it's in the mountains of Rwanda or the floodplains of the American South.

The world's most abundant futures may emerge from places that have too often been framed through a lens of scarcity. Scarcity is everywhere today—scarcity of community, of humanity, of empathy, of responsibility to each other and the earth. Yet these projects remind us to listen: across disciplines, across geographies, and across generations to uncover the links that bind us to one another and to the land. We have seen the pursuit of an abundant future. In the places that have the most to gain, we have seen increased access to health, education, and economic stability. Buildings are tools of dignity. Landscapes are acts of reparation. What has emerged is an architecture rooted in place. We have seen evidence of progress all around us.

To those who have joined us, taught us, and partnered with us—thank you. Let us now build this more abundant future together.

This book is the product of years of collaborative inquiry across disciplines and across continents. The opportunity to work together in shaping projects where architecture, landscape, and ecology are inherently intertwined has profoundly influenced our understanding of design's role in advancing justice and regeneration. The perspective offered in this book is grounded in this shared experience and in the belief that only through deep collaboration can we achieve the kind of abundance these projects pursued.

The title of this book draws inspiration from the studio Seeking Abundance—Designing Engagement and Experience for All, which Sierra co-taught with Jeff Mansfield at the Harvard Graduate School of Design. That course challenged students to reimagine abundance not only as ecological, but also as social, sensorial, and spatial, as well. The spirit of that studio, a commitment to justice through design that is reflexive, inclusive, and multisensory, infused our thinking and helped shape the ethos of this book and has become a source of ongoing dialogue within the firm in how we think about and aspire to a future of Abundance.

We are deeply grateful to our publishing partners at Axiomatic Editions, notably Ashley Simone, who believed in this project from the outset, and to our editor William Richards, whose thoughtfulness and clarity helped bring these stories to life. Maggie Stern has stewarded this editorial process with extraordinary care, ensuring that the vision for this book could be realized across dozens of collaborators.

This book is the product of five years of work, starting with the early efforts of designers Joelle Riffle and Alejandra Cervantes Enríquez, who played pivotal roles in shaping the book's original framework and compiling the projects that would become its foundation. We are especially thankful for the leadership of Chris Hardy, James Kitchin, Cilva Chen, Therese Graf, Emily Goldenberg, Patricia Gruits, and Andrew Brose, each of whom helped coordinate and guide the development of the chapters and featured projects.

We are grateful to our project partners. The team at African Wildlife Foundation demonstrated for us the importance of seeking harmony between our environment, animals, and humans at the Ilima Primary School, and beyond. Thank you to Tara Stoinski and the Dian Fossey Gorilla Fund staff and board for modeling what a truly reciprocal partnership can look like. Their global leadership in conservation was both inspiring and foundational to the campus we created together—one that now serves as a platform to inspire others toward a lifetime of conservation. Through close collaboration between teams at every level of our organization, this project reflected a rare alignment of mission, method, and ambition. The desire not only to build, but to track impact—ecological, educational, and social—sets a new bar for how built environments can advance biodiversity and become enduring models for regenerative design.

We'd like to extend special thanks to Maura Rockcastle, who has been a selfless and supportive collaborator since the design of the Butaro Hospital, helping bring landscape into MASS's DNA, and to the TEN x TEN team, key conceptual and design collaborators on the Fossey campus, amongst many others.

by
Sierra Bainbridge
and Alan Ricks

Acknowledgments

We are indebted to the external contributors whose essays, art, recipes, conversations, and other contributions sharpened and deepened the perspective of each chapter. These include Hanif Kara and Lesley Lokko, whose enduring support and leadership in the field have been a source of inspiration, as well as Sarah Mineko Ichioka, Anita Berrizbeitia, Kelly Alvarez Doran, Cedric Mizero, and Dieuveil Malonga, whose voices represent an essential dialogue between design, ecology, and social action.

The visual narrative of this book is enriched by the remarkable work of photographer Iwan Baan, who has been the most generous of collaborators to MASS over the last fifteen years, along with the beautiful work of Gaël Ruboneka Vande weghe and Chris Schwagga. Their ability to capture the people, places, and atmospheres of our projects lends this book its depth and humanity. We also thank Fred Swart for his art direction and graphic design expertise, which have shaped this book into a compelling and accessible visual artifact, as well as Pascale Vonier for her support in the design's production.

We are profoundly grateful to the funders who have enabled this work to flourish—especially those who have supported and nurtured our work in climate action, including Karen and Brian Conway, the Wagner Foundation, Crystal and Christopher Sacca, and the Autodesk Foundation. This book reflects their belief in architecture's power to cultivate justice and regeneration.

We would also like to thank our parents. Ron and Eileen Ricks, thank you for giving me the chance to explore the mountains of Colorado at a young age and for instilling in me an early sense of wonder that shaped a lifelong understanding that nature is something to protect and cherish.

To my father, Jonathan Bainbridge, a hermit, who is still teaching me to sit in nature, watch her closely, and to try to live simply within her bounds. And to my mom, Suzanne Pecore, a lifelong seeker, who exposed me to philosophies that helped me to understand that our lives are only of value if they are in service of all beings, and who, with her own hands, laid down highways so that I might have the freedom to choose how best to do so.

Of course, no project featured in this book would have been possible without the builders, artisans, and community members who imagined, constructed, and now inhabit these places. The structures at Ilima, RICA, and the Fossey Campus were not just designed for these communities— they were built with them. Thousands of individuals contributed labor, materials, and knowledge to bring these spaces into being. Their craftsmanship, care, and commitment are embedded in every line of this book.

We also wish to acknowledge and recognize the hundreds of MASS team members across our studios who, every day, advance this work and believe a just and beautiful future is ours to create. From researchers and architects to landscape designers, engineers, filmmakers, and fabricators, this book reflects their collective creativity and determination to serve communities through design.

Finally, we extend our deepest thanks to the readers of this book, whose curiosity and care are essential to its purpose. *Seeking Abundance* is not a conclusion, but a preface—a call to imagine and realize a future where people and the planet thrive in balance. We hope these stories inspire action, reflection, and renewed commitment to transform our built world and ensure that the next generation inherits a future shaped not by scarcity, but by the pursuit and possibility of Abundance.

Sierra Bainbridge seeks to create spaces of research, engagement, and collaboration where context-driven, impactful design solutions can emerge, supporting communities, institutions, and thought leaders working to address our most urgent challenges and inequities. Her practice is grounded in openness, curiosity, and optimism, shaped by deep interdisciplinary experience, and focused on delivering projects that demonstrate what is possible.

As a founder and senior principal at MASS, Sierra directs the Landscape Studio and Abundant Futures Lab. With a background in landscape architecture, ecology, and regional planning, she advances holistic, comprehensive, cross-disciplinary approaches to design regeneratively. From early work on the High Line and Freshkills Park to the Rwanda Institute for Conservation Agriculture and the Ellen DeGeneres Campus of the Dian Fossey Gorilla Fund, her projects reveal the power of design to catalyze ecological and societal abundance. Her work has been recognized for design excellence, research and analysis, and sustainability by the ASLA, AIA, COTE, and Cooper-Hewitt Smithsonian Design Museum Awards.

Sierra also works to evolve the design professions through teaching and service. She served on the Landscape Architecture Foundation Board, and continues as board emeritus. She received the Berkeley Rupp Prize for career achievement, serving as practitioner in residence '23–'25. Sierra is a creative educator, teaching landscape, architecture, and interdisciplinary graduate studios and seminars at the University of Pennsylvania, Harvard University, UC Berkeley, the Boston Architectural College, and the University of Rwanda. Sierra has also developed innovative curricula for programs such as the University of Rwanda's Faculty of Architecture, the African Design Center's Graduate Design Program, and RICA's One Health & Food Systems curriculum. She holds dual master's degrees from the University of Pennsylvania in landscape architecture and architecture, and a BA in architectural history and fine arts from Smith College.

Alan Ricks is a founding principal and co-executive director at MASS. Under his leadership, MASS has garnered international acclaim for its innovative approach to addressing global challenges through design. He continues to collaborate on and lead a diverse range of projects, and oversees a group of interdisciplinary teams that support design and research across the practice.

Alan regularly teaches advanced architecture studios, including at Harvard University and Yale University, where he was most recently the Louis I. Khan Visiting Professor. Alan has presented at universities, conferences, and events around the globe. He has written and produced films focused on the role of architecture in catalyzing social change. Chris Anderson, chief curator of TED, described his TED talk as "a different language about what architecture can aspire to be."

Alan was honored with an International Fellowship from the Royal Institute of British Architects in appreciation of his significant contributions to the field. He is also a member of the World Economic Forum's Young Global Leaders, a community working towards positive change and progress in various fields. The governor of Massachusetts appointed him to the Designer Selection Board to select firms for state-funded work, and during his two terms, he also served as chair. He is also a member of the Harvard University Design Advisory Council.

Alan holds a master of architecture from the Harvard Graduate School of Design. He earned his bachelor of arts from Colorado College, where he was also bestowed an honorary doctor of fine arts degree.

Biographies

Andrew Brose was a director in MASS's Africa Studio for nearly fifteen years, at various times leading advancement & business development in Africa along with design management of health, education, and housing projects throughout the continent, including the Ilima Primary School, Mubuga Primary School, Butaro Doctors' Housing, Rwinkwavu Village Housing, Manicaland Health and Education reconstruction, and the Delivering More Maternal and Newborn Health Program. Andrew now works as director of operations at Migoti Trading which seeks to improve agriculture and community transformation in East Africa and he continues to contribute to MASS projects across the continent.

Rachel Brose played a key role in documenting and coordinating remote African projects. She supported the Ilima Primary School in DRC, capturing every step photographically and helping the team adapt to local contexts. Her work ensures that project narratives remain grounded, community-centered, and visually compelling. Rachel's dedication helps connect diverse stakeholders through powerful storytelling and meticulous project coordination.

Regina Chen, senior principal of process & learning in Boston, uses design as a catalyst for social justice and community healing. Regina has fostered a culture of learning and mutuality both at MASS and in the field at large, developing processes that champion accountability and push the bounds of design excellence. Her diverse body of work, spanning community engagement, research, narrative development, and process design, is marked by the capacity for deep listening and for guiding partners towards asking the questions that drive meaningful impact.

Niels Datema, director of MASS.Made, works closely with artisans and manufacturers, encouraging them to explore possibilities and push the boundaries of the production process. Since joining MASS in 2019, Niels has played a pivotal role in developing MASS's furniture design studio. He has managed the production of over 16,000 products for several large-scale projects, including Norrsken Kigali House, the Rwanda Institute of Conservation Agriculture, the Ellen DeGeneres Campus of the Dian Fossey Gorilla Fund, and the 73rd FIFA Congress.

Martine Dushime, senior project manager in Kigali, oversees cost control and procurement for MASS's East African construction projects. Joining in March 2018, she managed budgets for education, conservation, and health facilities—including the African Leadership University campus—ensuring transparent, efficient delivery aligned with local economic contexts. She's a key liaison between finance, contractors, and design teams.

Jessi Flynn's background includes site planning, landscape design, and construction administration for several MASS projects, using the concept of One Health Design (that human, ecological, and animal health are inextricably intertwined), including the University of Global Health Equity, New Redemption Hospital Caldwell, Butaro Oncology Support Center, Nyarugenge District Hospital, Equal Justice Initiative's Memorial for Peace and Justice, and the Ellen DeGeneres Campus of the Dian Fossey Gorilla Fund.

Joe Christa Giraso, landscape designer based in Kigali, shapes resilient, biodiverse outdoor environments that nourish communities. She led landscape design and construction oversight for the Ellen DeGeneres Campus and Rwanda Institute for Conservation Agriculture. With a master of architecture in landscape architecture from Leeds Beckett University (Chevening Scholar) and a bachelor of environmental design from University of Rwanda, she mentors emerging Rwandan women designers.

Emily Goldenberg is a design director at MASS, focusing on engaging partners and project teams in the design process to develop design solutions that advocate for its users and prioritize the conservation and health of our planet. Emily is a designer, manager, and team-builder with over ten years of experience, and has worked across a diverse range of project typologies in conservation, education, and healthcare. She has contributed to a number of MASS projects, including the Ellen DeGeneres Campus of the Dian Fossey Gorilla Fund, the National Memorial for Peace and Justice, the New Redemption Hospital, and African Leadership University.

Rosie Goldrick was an engineering director based out of our Africa Studio, and led a diverse team of engineers in the design and implementation of innovative projects throughout East Africa. She supervised structural design and construction on a range of projects in Rwanda including RICA, Norrsken Kigali House, Ruhehe Primary School, and the One Acre Fund Headquarters in Kenya. She has expertise in seismic design and the use of nonconventional materials. Rosie has a first class master's of civil engineering and architecture from the University of Southampton. She is a Chartered Member of the Institution of Civil Engineers, a Corporate Member of the Institute of Engineers Rwanda, and sits on the Rwanda Standards Board Technical Committee for Civil Engineering and Building Materials.

Therese Graf, a design director in our Landscape Studio, is a landscape shaper and team leader who is passionate about the potential to support thriving ecosystems, communities, and places of inspiration. Therese works across MASS's studios supporting the design and development of projects in conservation and public memory, where she strives to create an embedded understanding of the systems and identities that make up a place. Therese has contributed to the development of the Rwanda Institute for Conservation Agriculture, the Ellen DeGeneres Campus of the Dian Fossey Gorilla Fund, the Norrsken Kigali House, the Harris County Remembrance Park, and other projects.

Patricia Gruits is a co-executive director and senior principal, supporting the strategy, development, operations, finance, design, and governance of the North American studios. Patricia's work as an architect and researcher is rooted in the possibility of shaping a more just, beautiful, and connected world. Her decade-long tenure has seen her working at MASS's Boston Studio and in the Africa Studio, where she led design teams on acclaimed projects, including the African Leadership University, the Ellen DeGeneres Campus of the Dian Fossey Gorilla Fund, and the Maternity Waiting Village. She co-authored the Purpose Built series, a set of tools for creating impact-driven design, and has implemented this approach to the design of housing, schools, and health facilities around the globe.

Chris Hardy, design director, leads the Building Integrity group, developing standards, tools, and resources that ensure each building throughout MASS's portfolio embodies technical excellence and reflects its mission. He has always enjoyed tackling large problems, with the motivating belief that technical innovation and craft traditions can be united in an architectural idea, and that design can support the global need for conservation. Chris has focused on complex projects and delivery methods, leading the design and construction of the Rwanda Institute for Conservation Agriculture, the Western Serengeti Research Centre, and the New Lots Branch of the Brooklyn Public Library, among others.

James Kitchin, is director of engineering and performance & provenance who oversees construction and design coordination on large-scale projects, and co-leads the MASS Abundant Futures Lab. He ensures efficient delivery and quality control, blending technical expertise with community engagement to realize MASS's mission of designing impactful and sustainable buildings. James is committed to fostering transparent communication and collaboration among diverse stakeholders to achieve lasting community benefits.

Anton Larsen, a principal in MASS's Africa Studio, embraces the disciplinary and cultural diversity of the teams he leads across multiple countries. With MASS, he has curated an extensive portfolio of transformative projects in the education, civic development, workspace, and affordable housing domains. Anton's work reflects his dedication to social and environmental justice and his deeply held belief that it takes inclusive collaboration to create spaces that are attentive to the needs and aspirations of the communities they serve. As an accredited EDGE Expert and AIA International Associate, Anton advocates for sustainable design within and beyond MASS.

Aimable Mukire, a structural engineer based in Kigali, leads design development and construction management for education and community facilities. His role emphasizes collaboration with local teams and stakeholders to create resilient, culturally relevant architecture aligned with MASS's impact-driven ethos. Aimable is dedicated to fostering sustainable community growth through designs that respond deeply to local culture and environment.

Adam Saltzman, a principal at MASS, currently leads MASS's Partnerships and Business Development team in Africa. With a strong focus on community-driven solutions, he integrates sustainable materials and local building practices to enhance resilience and accessibility across East African projects. Adam's collaborative approach prioritizes local knowledge and capacity building to ensure projects are meaningful and lasting.

Maggie Jacobstein Stern's work explores how we communicate layers of narrative, truth-telling, and meaning. She is interested in the ways that exhibitions and interpretation can be used to express the stories and issues of our time, allowing us to unveil rich layers of meaning and to create new points of connection. At MASS, Maggie leads exhibitions work in her role as a director on the Advocacy team. She has contributed to a number of projects in our Public Memory and Memorials Lab, notably the Gun Violence Memorial Project.

Jean Paul Sebuhayi Uwase is committed to architecture that drives social impact. Based in MASS's Africa Studio, Jean Paul is a principal who guides design projects from conception to construction while managing client relations and ensuring effective collaboration. His portfolio spans maternal and newborn health, healthcare, public memory, and higher education. Jean Paul is a member of the Rwanda Institute of Architects and is committed to advancing the professional standards in Rwanda.

Theo Uwayezu is a design director in MASS's Africa Studio. Theo's architectural practice is informed by a sense of social responsibility and a passion for innovative design that responds to the needs and aspirations of the communities he serves. He aspires to create equitable value across the supply chain of every design product. Theo contributed to the design and construction administration of the Ellen DeGeneres Campus for the Dian Fossey Gorilla Fund, the One Acre Fund Headquarters in Kenya, the Munini District Hospital, and the construction administration of the Mubuga Primary School.

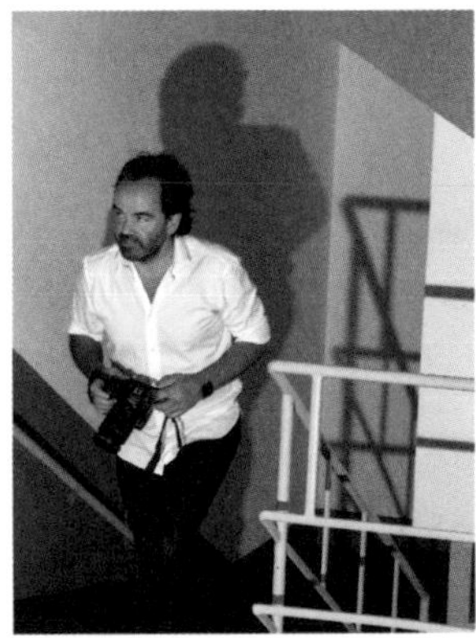

Iwan Baan is a Dutch architecture and documentary photographer based in Amsterdam. His photographs document the life of architecture around the world, from informal and traditional housing structures to the growth of megacities, and how individuals, communities, and societies reappropriate their built environment to make it their own. Baan has worked with leading architects and architecture studios such as Rem Koolhaas/OMA, Herzog & de Meuron, SANAA, Zaha Hadid, Steven Holl, and Tatiana Bilbao. His images are regularly published in newspapers and magazines such as the *New York Times*, the *Wall Street Journal*, the *New Yorker*, *Domus*, and *Architectural Digest*.

Anita Berrizbeitia is a landscape theorist and licensed practitioner, serving as professor (and former chair, 2015–22) of landscape architecture at the Harvard Graduate School of Design.

Berrizbeitia explores the relationship between ecology, technology, and culture in her scholarly and creative works. Born in Caracas, Venezuela, she holds degrees from Wellesley College and the Harvard GSD (MLA '87), and her award-winning publications include *Inside/Outside: Between Architecture and Landscape,* co-authored with Linda Pollak, and *Roberto Burle Marx in Caracas: Parque del Este, 1956–1961,* which received the J.B. Jackson Book Prize in 2007.

Kelly Alvarez Doran is a father, architect, and educator. His holistic approach to the design of the built environment has been shaped by his experiences working across the world—first in the resource development sector, and later as MASS Design Group's East African director where he led the design and implementation of several of MASS's projects, notably Munini District Hospital, One Acre Fund's Headquarters, the University of Global Health Equity, and the Rwanda Institute for Conservation Agriculture. In 2022 Kelly co-founded Ha/f Climate Design to provide environmental design strategy, education, and policy development. Over the past three years Ha/f has trained over 2,000 architects and co-developed policy with the City of Toronto and Federal Government of Canada. Kelly is an adjunct professor at the University of Toronto, a senior fellow of Architecture

2030, a founding member of the Bio-Based Materials Collective, and a member of the RAIC's Committee on Regenerative Environments.

Sarah Mineko Ichioka is an urbanist, strategist, curator, and author. She founded and helms Desire Lines, a studio that helps places, communities, and organizations chart paths toward thriving futures. In previous roles Sarah has explored the intersections of cities, society, and ecology within leading institutions of culture, policy, and research across the US, Europe, and Asia. Sarah's approach emphasizes inclusive planning processes that amplify marginalized voices and foster resilient urban ecosystems. She actively promotes cross-sector collaboration to create lasting social and environmental impact.

Hanif Kara, OBE, is a practicing structural engineer and professor in practice of architectural technology at the Harvard Graduate School of Design. He is passionate about linking design, research, education and practice. As co-founder of AKT II, his "design-led" approach has made him a pioneer solving challenges facing the built environment. Hanif's collaboration with MASS enriches projects by integrating cutting-edge structural innovation with social and environmental responsibility. He continually advocates for unbiased design solutions that address climate change while elevating architectural expression. His mentorship helps cultivate new generations of engineers (and designers from many fields) committed to sustainability, excellence in design, and equity.

Lesley Lokko, OBE, is an academic, novelist, and the founder and chair of the African Futures Institute, headquartered in Accra, Ghana. She is the recipient of the RIBA Royal Gold Medal 2024 and curator of the Venice Architecture Biennale in 2023. She was included in the 2024 annual TIME100 list of the most influential people in the world. She holds a BScArch, MArch, and PhD in architecture (UCL) and has lectured and published widely. She is a frequent contributor to international juries and awards, including the Aga Khan Award for Architecture (2016 and 2025).

Dieuveil Malonga is a chef, founder of Culinary Innovation Village, and owner of Meza Malonga, a culinary lab in Kigali, Rwanda. Born in Linzolo, near Brazzaville, Congo, Malonga was trained at Adolph-Kolping Schüle in Münster, Germany. He honed his culinary skills at Michelin-starred restaurants including Schöte, La Vie, and Aqua, and his work is guided by the spirit of Pan-Africanism, a celebration of unity of the peoples of Africa. Dieuveil's culinary innovation explores cuisine as a medium for storytelling and empowerment, and he is committed to celebrating African heritage and sustainable local food systems.

Cedric Mizero is a Rwandan multidisciplinary artist and storyteller whose work blends fashion, visual arts, and performance to explore themes of identity, memory, and cultural resilience. In October 2025, he will premiere his performative installation UMUNYANA at the Festival d'Automne in Paris, which interweaves fictional narrative with childhood reminiscences, focusing on themes of memory and mourning through the figure of the cow, a central element in Rwandan culture. His work has been featured in international exhibitions, including the Art of Peace: Art After War at the Art Gallery of Western Australia in 2025, and Protection at Crenshaw Dairy Mart in Los Angeles. Mizero's art continues to bridge personal and collective histories, offering profound insights into the human experience.

Maura Rockcastle is principal and co-founder of TEN x TEN STUDIO whose leadership approach is grounded in listening, questioning, and experimentation, allowing her work to translate experiences into landscapes through spatializing stories and activating the senses. Rockcastle balancess a rigorous approach to leadership and design innovation with a conceptual sensibility rooted in process. Her approach to designing landscapes grew from a lifelong fascination with ecologies, rocks, time, and art. Before finding landscape architecture, Rockcastle utilized printmaking and papermaking techniques to cultivate microlandscapes of mold and to observe deterioration over time. This ingrained passion for analog forms of thinking and making continues to guide her approach to designing landscapes.

Gaël Ruboneka Vande weghe is a Rwandan-based photographer, author, and conservation strategist whose work bridges nature, culture, and storytelling. Founder of Illume Editions, he has published acclaimed books on African biodiversity, including landmark works on birds and butterflies. His projects include high-value visual storytelling, immersive tourism experiences, and creative conservation initiatives across the continent.

Chris Schwagga (born Christian Mbanza) is a Burundi-born, Rwanda-based photographer who tells unique stories through various mediums, including photography, design, sculpture, costumes, and installations, exhibited globally. His work is driven by curiosity and he takes inspiration from people, travel, and culture. Chris's multidisciplinary creativity enriches MASS's narrative storytelling and helps illuminate the human stories behind each project.

Dr. Tara Stoinski serves as CEO and chief scientific officer for the Dian Fossey Gorilla Fund. Tara has studied gorillas for more than three decades and is the author of over two hundred scientific publications and books. Her work has been featured in *60 Minutes*, *National Geographic*, BBC, CNN, NBC, and *Wired*. Committed to training the next generation of African scientists, she recently co-led the creation of the Fossey Fund's award-winning Ellen DeGeneres Campus. She has been recognized as an Indianapolis Prize nominee, Women Making a Mark by *Atlanta Magazine*, and the Disney Conservation Fund's Trailblazing Women. Dr. Stoinski holds degrees from Tufts University, University of Oxford, and the Georgia Institute of Technology and is an associated faculty at Emory University. She also serves in leadership positions within the conservation, primate, and academic communities.

Ilima

Leadership	Sierra Bainbridge, Andrew Brose, Patricia Gruits, Michael Murphy
Team	Christian Benimana, Jonathan Bongi, Rachel Brose, Kelly Alvarez Doran, Patricia Gruits, Jeancy Mulela, Alan Ricks, Nicolas Rivard, Christopher Scovel, Jean Paul Sebuhayi Uwase, Christian Uwinkindi, Tim White, Regina Chen
Landscape Design	MASS
General Contractor	MASS
Structural Engineer and Sustainability Consultant	Arup
Mud-Construction Consultant	Scott Howard
Masonry	Ekongo Modogo, Ziko Lokuli
Carpentry	Camile Abiyo
Shingle Fabrication	Arthur Ilafa

Leadership	Sierra Bainbridge, Kelly Alvarez Doran, Rosie Goldrick, Chris Hardy, Anton Larsen, Alan Ricks, Adam Saltzman, Jean Paul Uzabakiriho
Architecture	Christian Benimana, Noella Nibakuze, Jean Paul Sebuhayi Uwase, Giovanni Bortolotti, Josh Greene, Taylor Klinkel, T.J. Burghart, Rene Gasana, Martine Dushime, Kelly Umutoni, Lamy Subira, Amani Rwibasira, Genna Kalvaitis, Jean Luc Ntwali, Catherine Lie, Erinn McGurn, Aziz Farid Shyaka, Bethel Abate, Symphorien Gasana, Nicki Reckziegel, Jamie Wiberg, Kristen Henderson, Deb Rosenberg, Anibal Niyitanga, Alba Mukundwa Karenzi, Ines Uwimbabazi, Nadia Perlepe, Alejandra Cervantes Enríquez, Giorgio Azzariti
Landscape Architecture	Jessi Flynn, Therese Graf, Jonathan Blaseg, Greg Dahlke, Patrice Uwizeyimana, Taylor Sinclair, Melissa Flatley, Joe Christa Giraso
Engineering	James Kitchin, Harriet Kirk, Cameron Bailey, Tilly Lenartowicz, Gilbert Hervé Ngenzi, Will Arnold, Claire O'Reilly, Nelson Habintwari, Obed Sekamana, Christian Uwinkindi, Andre Ntivuguruzwa, Shakira Nyiratuza, Okechi Opoko, Nadine Ishimwe, Sherryen Mutoka, Jacques Maniraruta, Aimable Mukire, Asyncrite Nyinganyiki, Serge Iradukunda, Darryl Tanner, Zani Gichuki, Munguakonkwa Taka Hubert, Richard Shumbusho, Paterne Niyonkuru, Clemence Twambazimana, Jean Damascène Sekamana, Jenny Kay
Furniture	Pim van Baarsen, Carissa Tan Tije, Paulien Nabben, Lotte de Raadt, Miguel Signes, Niels Datema, Christelle, Muhimpundu, Theophile Ndoreyaho, Jean Claude Kwitonda, Amie Shao, Maaike Hengeveld
Media	Thatcher Bean, Regina Chen, David Mutabazi, Gabriel Nyirijuru, Tracy Keza, Elsemieke de Boer, Joelle Riffle
Civil Engineering	Arup, MASS
Environmental Engineering	Transsolar
SMEP	MASS
Structural Engineering & Schematic Design	MASS, Arup
Contractor	MASS, Remote Group, Costwise
Quantity Surveying	MEW Consultants Ltd., Arabella
Graphics (presentations)	PEBL Design
Specifications	Conspectus

Construction

James Blackman, Binneman Menigo, Thierry Bucyana, Atif Rahman, Patson Marime, John Ruvugwaho, Jean Luc Shema Karuyonga, Irene Ishimwe, Otheniel Mwanyika, Pascal Gasana, Theodor Ndatimana, Theoneste Nkurikiyimana, Timothy Mruttu, France Kizungu, Maha Yassin, Agnes Mukamana, Alice Umulisa, Francoise Mukashyaka, Fred Taremwa, Rosyne Umuhoza, Alexis Habimana, Anathole Abimana, Pelagie Muhorakeye, Rodrigue Kalisa, Dieudonne Shimirwa, Edmond Kalimba, Nolaste Dushimerurema, Lawrence Ondimu, Rehema Niyitegeka, Leodomir Musanganya, Alain Tuyishime, Martens Hategekimana, Eustache Rutiyomba, Zawadi Barasa, Patrick Kayiranga, Janvier Rutsobe, Jean Claude Kalibu, Helen Ward, Azarias Kuradusenge, Pacifique Muhire, Aimable Twizeyimana, Robert Gahunde, Alex Ntirushwa, Justus Mwesigye, Amourani Cyiza, Esther Mushimiyimana, Didier Kalisa, Egide Yangiriyeneza, Emmy Ndinda, Fanwell Matope, George Birabamu, Herve Muheto, Innocent Barihonga, Jean Marie Vianney Bizimana, Jean Paul Hakizayezu, Kasompe Musonda, Samson Ntirushwamaboko, Sylvestre Habimana, Theoneste Tuyishimire, Tonny Makumbi, Yves Ndayishimiye, Jean Aime Niyonsaba, Leonard Twagirayezu, Ezekiel Kitayimbwa, Jean Marie Vianney Mutakirwa, Kent Rasmussen, Marie Godelive Mutegarugori, Yvanie Kamikazi, Claudine Ishimwe, Prince Rukeribuga, Alphonse Kanimba, Alphonse Nsengiyumva, Antoine Vita, Bonaventure Nizigiyimana, Delphine Umutoni, Deo Amini, Dieudonne Nzaramba, Digne Kamugire, Edison Nsabiyaremye, Elisa Bukura, Emmanuel Kamanayo, Epaphrodite Hakizimana, Eric Karambizi, Eric Mbanjineza, Faruk Salongo, Faustin Twizeyimana, George Wambongo, Hussein Ndayambaje, Janvier Muhire, Jean De Dieu Gahungu, Jean Thierry Bondo, Jeanne Muratwa, Joel Nshimiyimana, Jonathan Gakiga, Juliette Mukashyaka, Margret Matsiko, Olivier Nduwamungu, Rachidi Mazimpaka, Samson Hakizimana, Samuel Ssenkatuuka, Theoneste Bagambiki, Christian Munyaneza, Etienne Ahishakiye, Francois Ntigurirwa, Jacqueline Uwiragiye, Jean Paul Ndahimana, Alex Mugisha, Juste Abimana, Evariste mbarushimana, Seleman Havugimana, Jean De Dieu Ndengeyintwari, Yvonne Ingabire, Samuel Hazakirabenshi, Patrick Ukwishaka, Jean De Dieu Mahame, Rachel Umutesi, Pierre Ntawumvayino, Jim Owoyesigyire, Prosper Hatangimana, Issa Bikorimana, Jean Bosco Bimenyimana, Placide Munezero, Alice Mukahigiro, Moses Muvara, Elyse Uwitonze, Florence Mukashyaka, Charles Nsanzimana, Didier Shema, Naome Uwamubona, Felicien Irivuzimana, Emmanuel Rushema, Moise Niyongabo, Anaïs Ajeneza, Faustina Tuyambaze, Jean Nepomuscene Nsengimana, Jonas Nsengamungu, Protegene Harindintwari, Irene Mukarutabana, Venant Imanariyo

Project Teams

Leadership	Sierra Bainbridge, Emily Goldenberg, Patricia Gruits, Michael Murphy, Alan Ricks, Adam Saltzman, Theo Uwayezu
Design Team: Architecture	Bethel Abate, Giorgio Azzariti, Alex Dallas, Ana Fernandez, Victor Iyakaremye, Thandizo Kachiza, Lysette Niragira, Nadia Perlepe, Nicki Reckziegel, Youssouf Renzaho, Megan Suau, Annie Wang
Furniture	Amie Shao, Niels Datema, Miguel Signes, Christelle Muhimpundu, Jean Claude Kwitonda, Sylvie Dufitimana, Amani Rwibasira
Engineering	Aimable Mukire, James Kitchin, Nelson Habintwari, Cam Bailey, Rosie Goldrick, Herve Ngenzi, Jacques Maniraruta, Christian Uwinkindi, Harriet Kirk, Tilly Lenartowicz, James Musoni, Paterne Niyonkuru, Okechi Opoko, Asyncrite Nyinganyiki
Landscape	Therese Graf, Joe Christa Giraso, Taylor Sinclair, Greg Dahlke, Jessi Flynn, Andrew Younker, Jonathan Blaseg, Rachel Blaseg
Film & Media	Thatcher Bean, Elsemieke de Boer, Regina Chen, Tracy Keza, David Dusabirane, David Mutabazi, Brianne Nueslein, Gabriel 'Lucky' Nyirijuru, Joel Muhozi
Exhibit Design/ Wayfinding	Amie Shao, Maggie Stern, Bethel Abate, Miguel Roldan Signes, Joelle Riffle, Marisol Andrade Munoz, Morgan O'Hara, Christelle Muhimpundu, Martine Dushime, Amani Rwibasira
Impact	Regina Chen, Elsemieke de Boer, Veyom Bahl, Kemunto Okindo
Landscape Architect	Rachel Salmela, Ross Altheimer, John Rasmussen, Satoko Muratake (TEN x TEN) and MASS
Civil Engineers	MASS and Oak Consulting Group
Structural Engineer	MASS
M&P Engineers	MASS
Electrical Engineers	Buro Happold Engineering
Environmental Engineering	Transsolar
Construction	MASS
Constructed Wetland Consultants	Sherwood Design Engineers, Jacques Nsengiyumva
Furniture Design & Fabrication	MASS.Made, MASS
Exhibit & Wayfinding Design	MASS, Local Projects
Exhibit Fabrication	Formula D Interactive
Immersive Theater	Habitat XR
ICT & Security	Techno Engineering Company
Wayfinding & Signage	MASS
Media	MASS

Adobe Stock Images
119

Iwan Baan
80-81
98-99
100-104,107
182-183
187
188-189
190-191
193 (top and bottom)
195 (top and bottom)
197 (top and bottom)
199 (top and bottom)
201
208-209
212-213
221

Ronan Donovan for National Geographic Magazine
176-177

Bob Campbell Papers
*Special and Area Studies Collections, George A.
Smathers Libraries, University of Florida*
175

Dian Fossey Gorilla Fund
172-173

Super Local/Pim van Baarsen
140-141
142-143

Cedric Mizero
158-163

Philippe Nyirimihigo
64

Chris Schwagga
129
133
139
148-149

Gaël Ruboneka Vande weghe
12-13
14-15
16-17
58-59
60-61
62-63
66-67
68-69
74-75
164-165
166-167
168-169
230-231
232-233

Unattributed photos are courtesy of MASS

Contributor Photos
Iwan Baan: Vojtěch Veškrna
Gaël Ruboneka Vande weghe: Philippe Nyirimihigo
Lesley Lokko: Portrait by Alix McIntosh
Hanif Kara: Courtesy AKT UK
All others are courtesy of the contributor

Photo Credits